John Donnelly
The Knowledge

faber and faber

First published in 2011
by Faber and Faber Ltd
74–77 Great Russell Street
London WC1B 3DA

Typeset by Country Setting, Kingsdown, Kent CT14 8ES

Printed and bound by CPI Group (UK) Ltd, Croydon, CR0 4YY

A CIP record for this book
is available from the British Library

978-0-571-27672-1

The Knowledge

John Donnelly's plays include *Bone* (Royal Court Theatre), *Poll Tax Riots* (The Factory), *Corporate Rock* (Nabokov/Latitude Festival), *Conversation #1* (The Factory/V&A/Latitude Festival/SGP), *Showtime* (LAMDA), *The Kraken Falls in Llangollen* (Clwyd Theatr Cymru/Write to Rock), *Songs of Grace and Redemption* (Liminal Theatre/Theatre 503).

by the same author

BONE
SONGS OF GRACE AND REDEMPTION

For R

You held my hand at the water's edge that night.
If only we had swum together.

Acknowledgements

I thank the following.
There are more. I apologise. My memory

Charlotte Gwinner, Josie Rourke and all at The Bush;
Grant Davis, Paul Miller, Kate Wasserberg,
Stephen Unwin, Beth Byrne, Tony Clark, Frances Poet,
Simon Stephens, Chris Campbell, Dinah Wood,
Steve King, David Eldridge, Phil and Jay Knox,
the brilliant Lisa Foster and all at ABR; the staff
and students of the many schools who let me through
their doors, not least Amanda Wood, Steve Munday
and all at William Edwards

May we educate our children well enough
that they oppose our own folly

@UKuncut
@indoncensorship
@propershameful

Author's Notes

The play is set in various locations in and around Tilbury, Essex, in particular a secondary school.

Locations include a temporary (demountable) outdoor classroom, corridors, an office, a flat, a pub, a garden, and Tilbury Fort. As with physical actions, these settings are occasionally specified for clarity but in the main should be inferred.

A production should invoke, not replicate. Scenes and locations, while distinct in their playing, spill into one another. Characters often enter the preceding scene before it ends, perhaps never leaving the stage itself. Entrances and exits usually signify the beginning or end of a character's involvement with a given scene, not necessarily a literal entrance or exit. A sense of encroachment throughout.

Punctuation is for dramatic, not grammatical effect. Parentheses ( ) can indicate a change of direction of thought or addressing a new speaker. A slash / indicates the point at which the following character begins to speak. Much of the dialogue, particularly in the classrooms, is fast and overlapping. This should accentuate any pauses, which should be employed sparingly.

Tilbury is a shipping port situated on the Thames Estuary, with transport links to London as well as various international docks via the North Sea.

An interval may occur between Autumn and Spring terms.

Characters

Zoe
twenties, white

Daniel
fifteen, black

Mickey
fifteen, white

Karris
fifteen, white

Sal
fifteen (female), Asian

Harry
fifties, white

Maz
late twenties (male), Asian

THE KNOWLEDGE

'Uh, the reasons are obvious, and I don't have time to go into them right now.'

Terrence Malick, *Badlands*

knowl·edge (nŏl'ĭj)

noun

1. Familiarity, awareness, or understanding gained through experience or study.

2. Specific information about something (i.e. 'insider *knowledge*').

3. The *Knowledge*: the comprehensive *knowledge* of the streets of London that a fully qualified black cab driver must learn.

4. Carnal *knowledge.*

Autumn

Enter Zoe, Mickey, Karris, Sal, Daniel.
   Zoe has a list.

Karris Top Shop?

Zoe I'm –

Sal You shop at Top Shop?

Zoe I don't think this –

Karris Can't believe she shops at Top Shop

Mickey I can

Zoe Why not?

Karris You're a teacher

Zoe Not that much older

Mickey I believe you, miss

Zoe Thank you, okay –

Mickey Don't mention it

Zoe Okay, we're going –

Mickey What you getting all huffy at?

Sal 'Don't mention it', embarrassing yourself

Mickey Giving miss a compliment

Karris Miss, you got a boyfriend?

Zoe That's none of your business

Karris Have yer?

Mickey Miss, you lesbian?

Sal Can't ask that

Zoe What's your name?

Mickey What?

Zoe What's your name?

Mickey Daniel

Zoe You're Daniel Carter

Sal Miss, you married?

Karris Ain't got a ring

Daniel Such a dick

Zoe Next person to speak without raising their hand gets a detention.

Mickey Already got detention

Zoe Well, you can have one tomorrow

Mickey Then too. And the day after

Karris It's true, miss, he's got detention every day this week

Zoe Why?

Sal 'Cause he's an idiot

Karris Mr Baynes gave it him last day of term

Mickey And for what, for nada. I'm gonna make a complaint

Sal Uhh, div, you set off fire alarms

Mickey Violation of my human rights is what it is

Sal See what we have to contend with

Mickey What they gonna do, anyway, can't exclude me

Sal Yes they can

Mickey Heard old Harry Baynes talking, already kicked out too many people, what?

Karris She wants you to be quiet

Mickey How do you know?

Karris 'Cause that's what teachers mean when they stare

   Pause.

Zoe I would like you to tell me your names and nothing else (what is funny about that?)

Sal Miss, it your time of month? I ain't being funny, just asking a question

   Pause.

Zoe (*to Mickey*) Okay, Daniel –

Mickey Uh, call me gayboy

Daniel Why you got to be such a twat?

Mickey You hear that, that language is outrageous, I would like to make a formal complaint to the relevant authority

Zoe Is your name really Daniel?

Mickey Course it is!

Zoe Who's Daniel?

Mickey I'm Daniel!

Karris I'm Daniel!

Sal I'm Daniel!

Zoe (*to Daniel*) So you're Daniel?

Mickey No, I'm Daniel

Karris I see what you did, that was well clever. See that, she's well clever, I like her now

Daniel Yes, miss

Mickey Just call him gayboy, what, he loves it up the arse

Zoe I will not have homophobic comments in the classroom

Mickey You telling me gay people don't love it up the arse?

Zoe Not all gay people have anal sex

Mickey Most of them

Karris Lesbians don't

Mickey They do, I've seen it

Karris They got no dicks, dur

Mickey It's on my phone, I'll show you

Zoe I see that phone I'm confiscating it

Mickey I'm just saying a fact

Zoe Well, you seem to know a lot about it, Mickey

Mickey I know gay people like it up the arse

Zoe I must say that's very mature of you

Sal She's being sarcastic

Zoe No, no, I actually think it's very open-minded of Mickey to take such an active interest in the gay community

Mickey What's she blathering?

Sal A-hah! Shame, shame!

Mickey What's shame about that?

Sal You only know so much about being a gayboy because you are a gayboy, that's right isn't it, miss, you're saying Mickey's a gayboy?

Zoe That's not exactly the –

Sal Aha! Mickey's a gayboy! Mickey's a gayboy!

Zoe That's not the point I was –

Mickey Up yours, Osama

Sal Fuck you Irish, you fucking terrorist

Zoe Hey that's too far!

Sal IRA

Mickey That's original

Sal Yeah and Osama's not

Mickey Where d'you get that from, your dad?

Sal Where d'you get that from, your fat mum?

Zoe The point I am making is that anal sex is actually as common with straight people as it is with gay people

Karris My days, that is rank

Mickey Karris loves it up the arse

Karris Shut up, I never

Mickey It's a compliment! I actually respect a woman who takes it up the arse, shows she's liberated

Zoe This is supposed to be a citizenship class for GCSE-level students. A mature subject for mature people. But apparently we lack the maturity. If anyone here thinks they are not a mature person, they can leave now
    Right, I want you (where do you think you're going?)

Mickey Said I could leave!

Zoe No I didn't

Mickey Said anyone who's not mature can go now

   Enter Harry, Maz.

Harry He said that?

Zoe Yes!

Maz Cheeky shit

Zoe It's not funny

Maz No, it's not.

Zoe I don't know what I'm doing

Harry No one does. Your problem's not that you don't know what you're doing, your problem is they know that you don't know what you're doing

Maz What happened after that?

Zoe I said, you're telling me you're not mature?

Maz Never ask a closed question

Mickey I'm fifteen years of age and I'm in a fucking retard's class, course I'm not mature

Zoe Can we not use that word?

Mickey Retard or fucking?

Zoe Retard

Mickey Oh / so we –

Zoe Both, both, you can't say either

Karris He's always like this, miss, just showing off, think he likes you

Maz He's just showing off

Karris Miss, I'm cold

Sal Freezin' in here

Zoe (They're right though, there's wires hanging from the ceiling)

Karris Why we got to be out here, I hate the demountable, how we come we not got a proper class?

Sal 'Cause she's not a proper teacher yet

Maz Little bastards

Karris Can't say that!

Harry Don't get distracted

Zoe I am a proper teacher, thank you

Sal I heard you're a student teacher

Zoe I'm newly qualified, I'm not a student

Sal That mean you get the sack if you're shit?

Zoe No

Harry and Maz glance at one another.

Mickey Want us out the way so the bods can do enterprise week

Zoe (*about the glance*) (What does that look mean?)

Karris Shit, this

Mickey Case any real people see us mongs

Zoe Can we just –

Sal Speak for yourself

Mickey As if I'd speak for you, Christ, I don't even know your language

Sal I know you don't, my language is English, what's yours, Irish twat?

Mickey You hear this, miss, racial abuse?

Zoe Uh! Can we have the rest of the lesson in silence?

Mickey Miss, is Maz your mentor?

Zoe If you're referring to Mr Mahsood then, yes

Mickey D'you fancy him?

Zoe I don't think that's appropriate

Maz Get you

Harry Behave, they chop it off for less

Karris I'd shag him

Harry The horror

Mickey You'd shag anyone

Karris Wouldn't shag you. Not if you gave me a million pounds and a PlayStation

Mickey What and you think he'd touch you knowing where you been?

Zoe Hey

Karris Pressed his stiffy up against me

Zoe He did what?

Sal No way

Maz What?

Mickey This story's old

Karris It's true right, in PE he was showing me how to hold a hockey stick and he got a boner in his pants

Maz That is out of context

Zoe Out of context, is it?

Karris Felt it right up against me bum

Sal Right dirty bastard, Maz

Mickey See him down New York's with the dolly birds, gets some crackers

Zoe Should I be hearing this?

Karris Quite liked it

Zoe Okay

Sal You are so dirty

Zoe As you are incapable of obeying even the simplest instructions, it seems I have no choice but to get you copying out answers in silence for the remainder of the lesson

Karris This is well boring

Zoe In *silence*!

Mickey Stress factor

Harry Mindless repetition, that, and hyperbole, they're your base currency (I'm serious)

Maz The point is, Harry, she did alright. No riots, no walk-outs

Zoe I did do something stupid

Harry How stupid?

Mickey Miss, you teach English?

Zoe Yes

Mickey Are you very knowledgeable?

Zoe Well, I have a degree in English

Mickey So you're going to give us some of that knowledge, miss?

Zoe Is this relevant?

Maz Don't say yes

Zoe (How was I to know?)

Mickey I mean do you like that, miss, giving knowledge out, seeing as you're a teacher?

Zoe I suppose that is one of the things that attracted me to it, yes

Karris What, that you like giving out knowledge?

Zoe Yes

Mickey Is that something a teacher has to be good at, giving out knowledge? In your professional opinion

Zoe If they're going to be a good teacher, yes

Mickey Are you a good teacher, miss?

Zoe Well you'll be the judge of that

Mickey Aren't I the lucky boy?

Zoe Okay, what's going on?

Mickey Are you giving me knowledge now?

Sal So disgusting

Zoe What's so funny?

Mickey Nothing, miss, I'm as confused as you are. I'm just asking if you give good knowledge

Zoe What does knowledge mean?

Mickey Knowledge means knowledge

Sal Not funny

Mickey Just 'cause you're a virgin

Sal Just 'cause you're a slag

Mickey You flirting again?

Zoe What does knowledge mean?

Mickey You're the teacher!

Daniel It means shine, miss, you just said you were gonna give Mickey shine

   Beat.

Mickey She doesn't know what shine is!

Daniel Brains, head

Zoe Okay

Mickey Ahah!

Zoe I get it (thank you Daniel)
   I don't find it funny

Karris/Mickey Ooooh!

Zoe You are staying behind after the lesson

Mickey Why's that, miss? so you can give me knowledge?

   Exit Daniel, Karris, Saleema, Mickey.

Zoe So humiliating

Maz They're insecure

Harry Insecure? Oh yeah, that's *Guardian* reader for wanker, isn't it?

Maz It's a difficult group

Zoe There's only four of them

Harry There were only four horses of the apocalypse, I don't recall a queue to teach them citizenship

Maz They're not that bad

Harry Should have been out on their ear a long time ago, would have been if the acting shithead's job didn't depend on keeping the exclusion rate down

Maz Lose kids, lose money

Zoe Why am I teaching a subject I know nothing about to students who don't want to be here?

Harry The students you've got fall between two stools. they're either repeatedly absent, disruptive or both, but for some reason they seem to yo-yo back, like flies on – (I was going to say flies on shit but that makes us the shit). Anyway, the acting shithead thinks enterprise is something to aspire to, raising standards and blah, which is why your lot can't join late

Zoe So I'm babysitting them?

Harry I certainly didn't say that

Zoe How long for?

Harry Halfway through next term, then it's personal study, and don't start that crap about their home lives, Maz, I know their home lives are shit, but there's plenty of kids with as shit or shitter lives

Zoe Where can I get pens?

Harry Pens?

Zoe For the whiteboard

Harry The fuck you think we are? Rymans?

Zoe Must be a stationery cupboard here

Maz A stationery, a stationery cupboard, you say, that ring any bells with you, Harry?

Harry Now you mention it, Maz, I do recall a rumour that my predecessor organised an expedition to locate the stationery cupboard. Needless to say they never returned. There are reports they actually found it laden with enough A4, paperclips, board pens and flipchart paper to make Solomon weep. But, like Narcissus falling in love with his own reflection, so overwhelmed were they with this fabled trove they could not tear themselves away, and there they remain, skeletal fingers clutching clean foolscap

Zoe So there's no acetates for the OHPs

Harry We don't need acetates for the OHPs

Zoe Why not?

Maz Because the wonders of our new virtual learning environment render the humble overhead projector redundant

Zoe This is the virtual learning environment that hasn't been built yet and never will be

Harry This one. She will go far

    Pause.

Maz I hear English is going well

Zoe Where d'you hear that?

Maz Kids

Zoe Were you checking up on me?

Harry No

Maz Yeah

Harry Don't worry, they said nice things

Maz The boys fancy you

Harry Just the boys, Maz?

Zoe I'm not really going to fail am I? I mean, no one actually fails their NQT?

    Pause.

Harry It's very rare

Zoe I could fail?

Harry Let's not say fail, we don't need to use the word fail. Not at this stage

Zoe Oh my God!

Harry Look, can we just forget the word failure, put it right out of our heads, I don't think it's helpful, it has very negative connotations

Zoe Of failure

Harry Precisely

Maz Swap them with seven red? I'll take citz, it's more kids but they're no trouble

Zoe You think I can't handle them

Maz I'm just saying it's a big ask for –

Zoe A girl?

Maz An NQT

Harry He was going to say girl. That's blatant discrimination / I were you I'd sue the fucker

Maz (Piss off.) I'm not saying I'm a better teacher, just I've got more experience

Harry Stop patronising the poor girl

Zoe Stop patronising 'the poor girl'?

Harry I could have phrased that better

Zoe They're my class, I'll take them

Harry That's the spirit, we're all in this together (besides we can't swap, we're going to a split timetable). Look, just, y'know, inspire them

Zoe Now why didn't I think of that?

Harry Fill their sponge-like brains with the mysteries of knowing

Zoe Thanks, Harry, and afterwards, why don't I sort out climate change and the economy?

Harry As long as you get your marking done, can do what you like

Maz She could use The Smurf

Harry She's not ready for The Smurf

Zoe What's The Smurf?

Maz She's not ready for The Smurf

Zoe I'm glad I'm such a source of amusement

Maz So are we, it was dull till you showed up

> *Enter Mickey, Daniel.*
> *Exit Harry, Maz.*
> *Daniel picks up a book of poetry.*

Mickey How come he gets to walk around?

Zoe He's not in detention

Mickey So what's he doing here?

Zoe He wants somewhere quiet to work

Mickey What are you, a ventriloquist's act? Is he the dummy?

Daniel That's right, she's got her hand up my arse, making my tongue move

Zoe suppresses a laugh.

Mickey That'd be about right, I hear you like things up your arse, Danny

Daniel Grown-ups are talking

Mickey What, you a grown-up now?

Zoe Compared to you he is, yes
Read much poetry?

Daniel Some

Zoe Who do you like?

Daniel Larkin

Zoe Philip Larkin?
Sorry, I just –

Daniel My dad used to recite poetry, help me sleep

Mickey In the shed?

Zoe Ignore him

Daniel Had a really good memory. He was a cabbie, he knew loads

Zoe Do you write?

Daniel Sometimes

Zoe So do I. What do you write?

Mickey 'Dear Diary. Today I got bummed by three men with moustaches'

Zoe Is the bit of your brain that stops thoughts just tumbling straight out your mouth missing? Do you even think or just do stuff?

Mickey Want to know what I'm thinking right now?

Zoe No, get on with your work
   Alright, you got me, what?

Mickey Poling Kate Winslet up the bum. She's got the look like one of them posh birds who's mad keen for it. You know, on the surface all prim but in private, you know, I bet she'd, like, wee on your face and that, it's quite romantic

Zoe I find that disgusting

Mickey Actually miss, you look a bit like her

Zoe Do you want another detention?

Mickey Will you be there?

Zoe Only one way to find out isn't there, Mickey?

Mickey You asking me out? Sorry miss, you're not my type
   What you laughing at, gayboy?

Daniel Don't mind Mickey, miss, he got dropped on his head when he was a baby, never recovered. Think I'm joking, can still see the dent

Mickey Shut up

Daniel He's got a flat head, it's true

Mickey I have not

Daniel Miss, he's got a flat head hasn't he, you can see where it goes funny

Zoe Alright

Daniel Look close it looks like a spoon

Mickey Remind us, Danny, why arcn't you in the library? Oh I remember, it's because of the nasty names people call you

Zoe Okay

Mickey And you can't go home, why's that, 'cause your mum's probably passed out on the kitchen floor, waiting for Daddy to come home

Daniel steps up to Mickey.

Go right ahead, I'm fine with that

Zoe Daniel, sit down. Daniel, sit down

Mickey Daniel, sit down. Daniel, sit down

Daniel sits down.

Zoe Ten minutes. Please, I need to get these reports done

Mickey Lighten up

Zoe Do not tell me to lighten up. I don't need to lighten up

Daniel Could lighten up a bit, miss

Zoe Don't start with me
     Be good to hear one in class sometime, Daniel, one of your poems

Mickey Thought you had reports, now you're starting a conversation

Zoe I'm talking to Daniel, not you

Mickey Such a hypocrite

Daniel Yeah, I'll do one

Zoe Great

Daniel If you give me a kiss

Mickey What the fuck?

Zoe I don't think that's appropriate, Daniel

Daniel I was joking

Zoe All the same

Daniel It was a joke, I'm sorry

Mickey How come he says that and he doesn't get shit?

Zoe It was a joke, Mickey, a bit misjudged, but a joke, that's all

Daniel Sorry, miss

Zoe He just apologised, okay, that's the difference

Mickey That was me I'd be in so much shit

Pause. Mickey stares at Zoe.

Zoe Mickey, would you mind not staring at me

Mickey I wasn't staring. Must have imagined it

Zoe tries to work. Mickey continues to stare. She looks at him.

'S it bother you me looking at you?

Zoe Have you finished your work?

Mickey Why don't you come over here and look at it? Now who's staring?

Zoe Bring your work to me

Mickey No

Zoe I said bring me your work

Mickey Dog ate it

Zoe Your dog ate the work you've been doing the last forty-five minutes

Mickey Yep

Zoe Where's your dog?

Mickey You want to see my dog? Sure. He's friendly. You can stroke him

Zoe I don't like your tone of voice

Mickey I like yours

Zoe I'll be talking to Mr Baynes about this

Mickey Why, for pretending I had a pet dog? That's a crime these days? Having a bit of a joke and a laugh

Zoe That wasn't what you were doing

Mickey What was I doing?

Zoe You were implying something else

Mickey What?

Zoe You were implying something else when you talked about your dog

Mickey I was just pretending I had a dog. Why, what did you think I meant? What did you think I meant? Some people have got funny minds

Zoe I think it's time you left, Mickey

Mickey Detention's not over

Zoe It's over when I say it is

Mickey What, you think you're in charge out here?

Zoe I'm the teacher, Mickey, that's how it works

Mickey Two against one, miss, what are you going to do about it?

Zoe What do you mean by that?

Mickey Nothing

Zoe 'Two against one, miss' – what does that mean?

A long pause.

I think you should go

Mickey You're pretty forceful, miss

Zoe I'll be speaking to Mr Baynes about you

Mickey Whatever turns you on

Exit Mickey.

Zoe It's probably time you went, Daniel

Daniel Want me to walk you to your car?

Zoe Why would I want that?

Daniel So you feel safe?

Pause.

Zoe No, I'm fine, thank you, Daniel

Enter Maz, Harry.
Exit Daniel.

Harry You've got thirty kids in your class, twenty-five who turn up. Five shitheads, fifty per cent of your time goes on stopping them setting fire to each other

Maz What's this, a pep talk?

Harry Another five who have a brain and might actually get somewhere and half-a-dozen sweethearts whose curse in life is to be average (the fuckers) –

Zoe These bloody heels, my feet

Maz Don't wear 'em then

Zoe They tower over me in flats

Harry They're the ones you want to help, the ones you could help, but you haven't got the time because you spend half your life trying to pander to kids who, and

I know you don't like to hear this Maz but it's true, we're wasting our time with

Zoe 'Cause every child matters

Harry You know the problem with people like you?

Maz Harry's had a drink

Harry You think the world is this happy liberal place where democracy works and everyone is reasonable

Zoe Did you just say you don't believe in democracy?

Harry Two years from now, Mickey O'Shea is eligible for jury service. Mickey O'Shea. Picture it, you're in the dock, you look up and your future rests on Mickey's ability to pay attention for more than eight seconds. There's your democracy. And that's for the round

Harry leaves a banknote.

Zoe I need to talk to you about Mickey O'Shea

Maz Good luck in his state

Harry Everyone needs to talk to me about Mickey O'Shea, my whole life is one long conversation about Mickey O'Shea

Maz He's alright

Zoe He said something

Harry What else is new?

Zoe He made a threat

Maz A threat?

Harry What kind of threat?

Zoe I don't know if it was a threat

Harry Was it or wasn't it a threat?

Maz Harry

Harry Says he made a threat

Maz What did he say?

Zoe He was in detention with Daniel Carter, and I said something to him and he said 'Two against one, miss, what are you going to do about it?' Or something like that

Harry Or something like that

Zoe I'm pretty sure that's what he said, words to that effect

Maz Words to that effect?

Zoe Yeah

Harry And that's the threat?

Zoe It was the way he said it

Maz What do you think he meant?

Harry Could have meant a lot of things, really

Zoe I know it doesn't sound – but look, in the demountable you do feel a bit isolated

Harry If you want an easier group just say

Zoe No, it's not –

Harry I thought you were making progress, but –

Zoe I'm not after an easier –

Harry Mean if it's too much –

Maz Harry

Zoe It's not too much

Harry 'F you're overwhelmed

Zoe I'm not overwhelmed

Harry You're sure? I mean, say if you are, I'm not putting words in your mouth, you're sure?

Zoe Yes

Maz Could always use The Smurf

Zoe Oh fuck off with The Smurf

Harry Look, I'm half pissed

Maz Half?

Harry If you're bothered, write it up, shove me an email. Oh! Staff Christmas party

Maz You going?

Harry Course she's going, she's organising it

Zoe Since when?

Harry Since now. Talk to Sheila in the office

Zoe I haven't got time

Harry No one's got time, Zoe, but somehow things happen

Zoe Any advice?

Harry Yeah, don't go to bed with him

Zoe About the party?

Harry Don't go to bed with him.

Maz Piss off

Harry Harry's parting thought: I know this one may seem like a charming scamp, but he will try and fuck you and no good will come of it

Maz Don't believe a word this frustrated / old queen says

Harry It'll seem like such a great idea / then come the morning –

Maz He's been trying to shag me for years

Harry – there'll be a lot of awkwardness in the staff room

  Exit Harry.

Zoe Still haven't got any pens

Maz Listen, if you want to swap classes

Zoe You think I can't handle it

Maz I never said that

Zoe I can't fail this, I'll have to pay back my tuition fees. Can't have my parents bail me out again, enough of a fuck-up as it is in their eyes

Maz You won't fail

Zoe Harry doesn't seem to think so

Maz He's just trying to keep you on your toes

Zoe Well, it worked, I feel completely out my depth.
  That's your cue to say, 'You're doing fine'

Maz 'You're doing fine'

Zoe Hand my planner in a day late, the most almighty shitstorm, mention a student sexually threatens me I'm 'making a thing of it', I don't get it
  It's the weekend and we're talking about school!

Maz Let's talk about something else

  A long pause – what else is there to talk about? They laugh.

Zoe So, you and Karris Jones

Maz Lies, all lies

Zoe Well that's funny because she told me you practically shoved your cock up her arse in a PE lesson

Maz She can't go round saying things like that, she'll get me on a register

Zoe She didn't sound too emotionally scarred by the experience I have to say

Maz Look, about a year ago

Zoe Ha!

Maz What?

Zoe Look at you, you're bloody dying to tell me!

Maz I am not!

Zoe Get on with it

Maz I covered a PE lesson and we were doing hockey. And most of them they wear (fuck off it's not funny), most of them they wear tracky bottoms, but Karris Jones is wearing this pair of shorts that I swear barely covered her arse

Zoe Oh, so she was asking for it?

Maz Just listen, right, so at one point she calls me over and says, sir, can you show us how to do a proper grip. So I go over. And I'm standing behind her, with my hands over hers, showing her this hockey grip, and she just slides her arse back into my groin. And I swear I was not thinking anything

Zoe Oh yeah right

Maz I couldn't help it, I just got this full mast lob on, no listen, right, I was trying to adjust myself so I wasn't touching her, but she kept backing into me

Zoe I'm now imagining you saying this in court

Maz And by this point, I had this hard on so I could hardly walk away from her, with a – look, I defy any man under the circumstances to say different. I just had to keep moving me groin away and thinking about you know, dog shit, and snogging your granny and all that

Zoe Oh my God

Maz Anyway, finally it goes and I said, okay, I'd better go and help some of the other girls, and she just looks at me, like . . . And says, thanks sir, you're a really good teacher. I swear

Zoe No!

Maz I did not fucking try and bum her, right, for the record I derived no pleasure from the whole incident

Zoe You're telling me you had Karris Jones in tight shorts, grinding her arse into your cock, you had a hard on and you got no pleasure from it?

Maz Look, I can't –

Zoe I'm turned on by Karris Jones in tight shorts

Maz Didn't know you went that way

Zoe She looks amazing, you don't have to go that way to see that. Just feel past it next to her

Maz You're hotter than Karris Jones

Zoe Shut up

Maz I would

Zoe Hush

Maz I mean it

Zoe I know you do, I know how you spend your weekends

Maz Don't believe everything you hear

Zoe Oh come on

Maz Make it sound like I'm some kind of menace. Yes, I sometimes have sex with adult women

Zoe Adult! I've been to New York's

Maz They've got ID

Zoe You check?

Maz I have done – what? *What?*

Zoe You're telling me, you saw Karris Jones in a nightclub, you didn't know her, and she came on to you, you'd say no?

Maz She's fifteen and she's a student at a school where I teach

Zoe One year from now, she's left school, she's not in your care, she's sixteen. You'd say no?

Maz Would you ever go with a woman?

Zoe You changing the subject?

Maz Answer the question

Zoe No

Maz Course I'd fuck Karris Jones, have you seen her?

Zoe Can't believe you said that!

Maz Your turn, come on, I fessed up, now you, would you go with a woman?

Zoe Often when confronted with the miserable dumping ground for mankind that is the male of the species, the thought does occur

Maz Someone broke your heart

Blimey, someone did, di'n't they? Who, tell me, I'll hunt the bastard and kill him

Zoe My fiancé cheated on me

Maz The fool

Zoe With my sister

Maz Fucking hell

Zoe What's worse is her husband threw her out, my mum and dad took her in, then when I needed somewhere to stay, they said it was awkward. Now I don't talk to any of them. I had a job in London, on our doorstep, I just had to get away. This was the only place I could . . .

Maz The kingdom of the dispossessed welcomes you

Zoe It's so weird. The corridors, the smell, it does something to you

Maz See, this is what you need to let out in class

Zoe What?

Maz Life. You. They need a human being not an automaton

Zoe I'm a robot now?

Maz Just saying, drop the ice maiden – let it spill out a bit, let go, that's all

Zoe You are something else

Maz I have been told
    We could get a cab
    I'm serious

Zoe That's what worries me

Maz I know what you want

Zoe Great, I've been wanting to know myself, could you tell me?

Maz You want to feel special, like you're the only one that matters

Zoe (*gasps*) Are you psychic?

Maz You're funny and you're clever and you're passionate and you have integrity

Zoe Harry wasn't lying, was he?

Maz I mean this with the greatest respect. I would dearly like to spend the night with you

Zoe I've got reports

Maz So if you didn't have reports, you would?

Zoe What do you know about Daniel Carter?

Maz Are you changing the subject now?

Zoe He writes poetry

Maz Oh yeah?

Zoe I said would you read some out in class, he says I will if you give me a kiss. Don't laugh!

Maz Sounds like he knows exactly what he's doing

Zoe Seriously, he gets all this shit from Mickey, and – I don't know, he's so contained, he's like a cat

Maz A cat?

Zoe This energy like one day he's just gonna . . . go

Maz Sounds like you're starting to care

Zoe I fucking doubt it and would it be such a bad thing if I did?

Maz It's the doctors who care are the ones that kill, they get nervous

Zoe Don't worry about me, I'm in it for the holidays

Maz One more?

Zoe I've got a scheme of work to plan

Maz One drink

Zoe As long as you promise to behave yourself?

Maz Yeah, well, do you, that's the question?

Zoe gives Maz a stern look.

Alright, miss.
Fine, swear on the Bible!

Zoe I thought you were Muslim?

Enter Mickey, Sal, Karris, Daniel.
Exit Maz.

I don't think we got off to a great start. I think something
went astray. So up until Christmas, I'd like us to try
again. I don't feel I know you very well so I'd like you all
to tell me something about yourselves

Sal Miss, you look all tired and you got a sad face, d'you
have a late one?

Zoe Maybe say something about what you want in life.
Doesn't have to be long
Okay, my name's Miss Curtis, I teach English, I –

Sal Miss had a late one

Beat.

Zoe I like writing stories. Who wants to go next?
Anyone?
One of you?

Pause. Karris puts her hand up.

Karris! Great

Karris Miss, can I go toilet?

Zoe Wait until the end

Karris But I really need to go

Zoe You'll have to wait

Karris But miss, I'm cold

Zoe You're always cold. Someone must have something to say? Daniel?

Sal What are we supposed to say?

Zoe Anything! Just something that tells me something about you, something that means something, something you care about

Sal Like what?

Zoe I don't know

Sal Well if you don't know, how are we supposed to know? You're the teacher

Zoe But I'm not you, am I?

Sal Dur! Why d'you want to know something about us anyway?

Zoe So I can get to know you?

Sal Why?

Zoe So we can get on better

Daniel All this get-to-know-each-other shit
   We all know we're here 'cause no one knows what to do with us

Zoe I know the feeling
   Look, what is it that you want? In life?

Mickey Be a pop star

Zoe A pop star?

Mickey Or a lumberjack, I ain't fussy

Zoe Why a lumberjack?

Mickey I like trees

Zoe Please! I'm asking for your help.
  What am I doing wrong?

Daniel You ask us about us you need to tell us about you

Zoe I did, I told you I wrote stories

Daniel Something proper. It's all on your terms

Zoe Like what?

Mickey How old were you when you lost your virginity?

Zoe I'm not answering that

Mickey You have lost it though?

Zoe No, Mickey, I've never had sex, I've never had fun

Daniel See that's it, bit more personality

Zoe I'll answer sensible questions

Karris What kind of food do you like?

Zoe Italian

Karris Ah, I love Italian, miss likes same as me

Sal Where you from?

Zoe I'm from – well, I'm from Bournemouth but I
moved to London when I was seventeen

Karris What's it like, London?

Zoe You've never been to London?

Karris No

Zoe It's half an hour away on a train

Karris So?

Zoe Big

Karris What about the big wheel, you been in that?

Zoe I have actually

Karris London Dungeon, you been there?

Zoe No

Sal I went with my family once, it was wicked, they have this wicked ride at the end

Karris Why d'you move here, miss? I'd never move here if I lived in London

Zoe I had my reasons

Mickey What are they?

Zoe Well, if you must know, I broke up with my fiancé

Karris Oh, that's so sad

Sal Was he a shithead, miss?

Zoe Yes, he was actually, I'm better off without him

Karris You go girl! Was you clever when you was at school, I bet you was a right brainbox

Zoe No, I was always in trouble

Karris Really, what kind of things?
  Go on, miss, you can tell us. Smoking cigarettes? Was you a secret smoker?

Zoe Might have been

Sal D'you smoke weed?

Zoe I'm not answering that

Karris That's a yes

Zoe I didn't say yes!

Karris I know, but you got a cheeky grin though, gosh you was a right little tearaway

Mickey I got a question

Zoe Go ahead, Mickey

Sal It's gonna be a stupid one I can tell

Mickey What made you want to be a writer?

Zoe I don't know. I guess I – it was a way of expressing a part of myself I couldn't express any other way

Mickey Can you buy anything you've written?

Zoe No, I've had some short stories published in magazines, but that's it

Karris Really?

Mickey D'you get paid for them?

Zoe No. Student magazines

Mickey Like the school newsletter?

Zoe University

Mickey Nothing professional though?

Zoe No

Mickey So it didn't really work out then?

Zoe Well, I'm still . . . I still write

Mickey So what's this then? This just to tide you over till the writing takes off, is it?
Little stop-gap. Or is it research?
Or were you just not good enough?

Pause.

Sal Oh my days

Karris That is well rude
  Miss, you alright?

Sal Looks like she's gonna cry

Karris You are such a wanker

Mickey I just asked a question

Zoe Will someone please talk about themselves?

Mickey Not my fault she can't handle the pressure

Karris That is well out of line

Sal Such a little twat

Zoe *Will someone say something?*

  Silence.

Daniel Start Kensal Rise tube. Leave on the right,
Chamberlayne Road. Left Harvist Road. Forward
Brondesbury Road

Karris Oh my God, he's lost it

Daniel Right Kilburn High Road, see that pub corner
Willesden Lane, used to collect for the IRA, wankers, oh
pardon me, your Uncle Paddy, you say? Sorry darlin'
(should have noticed the rosary)

Mickey Fuck is this?

Daniel Left Belsize Road. Right Abbey Road, studios on
the right, oh here we go, four barefoot Japs blocking the
way. That must be Paul-san, there's John-san, George-
san, Ringo-san. Hang on, Ringo's a bird!

Karris What?

Daniel C'mon, it's a crossing, you use it to cross! Very
hard-working people the Japanese. Shame about the war.

Forward Grove End Road. Left St John's Wood Road, Lord's cricket ground on the left, see that flat, with the blinds, yeah, that's the one, two Swedish models used to live up there

Karris Did they!

Daniel Don't ask me how I know, just don't tell the old girl. Comply Roundabout. Left by the Prince Albert, piercings at the bar while-u-wait. Right Regent's Park Inner Circle (say no more). Set down on the right. And here's the Zoo. They got lions, elephants, zebras, giraffes, big cats, small cats, meerkats, monkeys, deer and two pandas: one female (gagging for it), one male (queer). Twelve pound, darlin'

Beat.

Mickey What was / that?

Karris That was amazing!

Sal That was wicked, man, what was it?

Daniel It's called a run, you have to learn 'em if you drive a cab, there's about three hundred and fifty. They're in this red book, which is called the blue book

Mickey That makes no sense at all

Karris You know them all?

Zoe I don't think he knows them all, Karris

Daniel Takes three years to learn them all, I only know a couple

Mickey Waste o' time

Karris What was all that stuff about Paul-san and that, that was well funny?

Daniel That's the Beatles

Sal Who are they?

Mickey You don't know who the Beatles are?

Sal Did your dad teach you?

Mickey What, before he left?

Sal No, after he left, dickhead

Mickey Look at me, I know some roads

Karris Oh my God, I could never remember all that, I get lost going home

Daniel Ain't just about remembering it. See when they test you, they don't just test you on the set runs, you got to know how to get from any place to any place, you got to *know* it. Keep everything on the oranges and lemons and you'll be fine, that's what he'd say

Karris What's oranges and lemons?

Daniel Colour of the roads on an A to Z. It means as long as you know the main roads, you can work out the rest

Zoe Oranges and lemons, I love that

Karris When you was doing it, you was moving your hands

Daniel It's what my dad used to do. When I was little and I couldn't sleep he'd put me in his cab and take me up London. He'd put me on his jacket, next to him where the luggage goes and 'cause I was too little to see out the window, he'd describe it all to me but like he was painting a picture

Karris Oh my days, that's so cute

Daniel So like Harvist Road would be like these big fields of corn or Kilburn High Road this wide country lane, just heading out to nowhere

Mickey My auntie lives in Kilburn it's a shithole

Sal Using his imagination, dur

Karris That was well good, wa'n't it, miss?

Mickey What about GPS? What's the point of knowing it when you got GPS?

Karris Don't be a dick

Mickey It's true, you don't even need to know any of this, waste of time you ask me

Sal No one did

Zoe Sometimes it's just good to know things, you don't always need a reason

Mickey Stupid

Sal Has it got a name?

Daniel The Knowledge

Mickey Oh my gosh you are joking. The Knowledge! That is sincerely classic. I've been given the Knowledge by gayboy

Sal You've done that joke, get over it

Zoe Mickey, taxi runs have been called the Knowledge for over a hundred years

Mickey People have been giving blowjobs for even longer

Karris God, their knees must be killing

Mickey And all that stuff about the IRA, that was just racist

Zoe It was a joke, Mickey

Mickey Well I don't think that's funny, that's racist against Irish people

Sal Shut up

Mickey Discrimination

Karris I think it's well impressive

Mickey What do you know?

Karris Jealous much?

Mickey Of him? Jealous of gayboy and his pisshead old lady

   Daniel stands up.

Zoe Daniel, don't rise to him

Mickey You want to bring it? I'm open to offers

Sal Lamp the twat

Mickey Like to see him try, little queer

Zoe Will you shut your spiteful little mouth

Mickey Fuck off

Zoe What did you just say?
   Would you like to repeat what you just said?
   No, I thought not, now –

Mickey I said fuck off. You ridiculous woman

Zoe Get out

Mickey No

Zoe I said get out

Mickey I heard you the first time

Zoe I told you to get out

Mickey And I told you I heard you. What, you fucking deaf? Fucking failed writer, you're a terrible teacher, worst I ever had, wasting our time with this shite

Sal Miss, you're not gonna get kicked out are yer? Someone said you were, that's not true is it?

Zoe Who said that?

Mickey You're a laughing stock. You're a joke, you're only here 'cause they don't trust you with proper classes

Zoe That's not true, I'm a good teacher

Mickey You're just pissed off 'cause you got dumped by sir
   Don't think we don't know. He told some year elevens in his football team he shagged you

Karris Miss, did you shag Maz?
   Nice one, miss, sir's well fit

Mickey What's the matter? Tears is it?

   Zoe exits the classroom. Daniel follows.

That's it, gayboy, running after your girlfriend

Sal How can he be a gayboy and her boyfriend? Idiot

Mickey Shut up

Sal Shouldn't have done that

Mickey Fuckin' deserved it

Karris No she didn't, that was well tight

Mickey What you staring at?

Sal You, wanker

   Zoe enters the staff toilets. Daniel follows.

Zoe Daniel, you can't come in here, it's the ladies. Please, go away

   Maz enters the classroom.

Mickey It was just a joke, anyway, she can't even take a joke. I didn't mean to say it, I just got angry, she knows I can't not say things when I'm angry, it's her fault
 Fuck this

 Mickey exits the classroom.

Maz Oi! What's going on?

Sal Mickey was really rude to miss and she started crying and ran off and Daniel went after her

Maz No one leaves this room

 Maz exits the classroom.

Zoe I can't do this

Daniel He's like this with everyone

Zoe Thank you, Daniel, but you need to go

 Daniel presents Zoe with a handwritten poem on a sheet of paper.

Daniel Thought maybe you could have a read, let me know what you think

Maz Miss?

 Maz enters the toilets.

Zoe He was just seeing if I was alright

Maz Thanks, Daniel, might be best if you go back to class

Zoe Not if Mickey's still there

Maz He's gone

Karris Feel like a right lemon

 Karris exits the classroom.

Maz Come on, Daniel, off you go

Daniel exits the toilets.

Zoe Think they're still there?

Sal exits the classroom.

Maz Course

Daniel enters the classroom. Surveys the empty room. Exits.

Zoe I work eighty hours a week and the holidays. That's a joke, I spend all my time planning or asleep I'm so knackered
  All my friends are in London
  Can't even go running any more 'cause of little pricks like this lot whistling and jeering, making animal noises
  For a few moments, I thought they liked me
  I'm not letting them beat me. I won't

Maz D'you ever get those pens you were after?

Zoe Did you tell students you fucked me?
  Mickey said you told your football team

Maz And you believe him?

Zoe Did you?

Maz Some year eleven lads (no wait), some year elevens had seen us arguing, they asked if I'd shagged you, I told them it was an inappropriate question

Zoe So you didn't deny it?

Maz If you deny it, it makes it worse

Zoe I can just imagine. 'Oh no, boys, you know me' – tipping them a little wink, lads together

Maz I'll tell them nothing happened

Zoe Oh that'll help. 'Just so you know, boys, I didn't shag miss'

Maz Look, they're not stupid, they saw us arguing

Zoe So it's my fault?

Maz Next term I'll take them, alright. We'll sort something out

Zoe You're worse than my bloody family
   Fucking master of the dark arts and here's me playing at being a teacher like a little girl with a dressing-up box

Maz You've had a shit day, that's all. Come on, we'll sort this out then we'll have a drink

Zoe And what is a drink exactly?

Maz It's whatever you want it to be

   Zoe laughs.

Zoe You're actually –

Maz I didn't mean . . .

Zoe I've got one more observation before Christmas
   Don't do me any favours. I don't need your help

   Zoe exits.
      Maz exits.
      Enter Mickey, Karris, Sal, Daniel.
      Zoe enters with a box from which she produces a blue prosthetic penis.

Mickey What you doing later?

Karris Avoiding you

Mickey What, with your big druggie friends at the gates?

Sal Oh my gosh!

Karris My days!

Mickey The fuck is that, looks like a Smurf?

Maz enters.

Maz Sorry, I'm –

Mickey Miss brought in a dildo

Zoe It's not a dildo, Mickey

Maz Ignore me

Zoe We will

Mickey I've seen a dildo, and that's a dildo

Sal How come you seen a dildo?

Mickey 'Cause I was looking in gayboy's bag?

Karris Come to see miss, sir?

Zoe No, he's come to see you, Karris, he can't keep away, someone with a sensible answer?

Sal It's a rubber dick

Zoe No it's not a rubber d— Well, actually, yes it is, but we're going to call it a prosthetic penis

Mickey Why's it blue?

Zoe I think so people from different races aren't offended

Sal What races got blue dicks?

Karris Eskimos?

Zoe passes condoms to Karris who hands them out.

Zoe Okay, pass these round

Mickey Got any extra large?

Sal Looks like an alien

Mickey parades around holding the prosthetic to his groin.

Mickey It's ET's dick! ET phone home! ET phone home!

Zoe Mickey, sit down

Mickey Ell-i-ot! Ell-i-ot!

Zoe Can we get through one lesson without the gratuitous commentary?

Karris What's 'gratuitous'?

Mickey leaves the prosthetic with Daniel.

Daniel He is

Sal I don't want them

Zoe Just to look at, don't need to keep them

Mickey Against her religion, miss

Zoe I don't think it's against Sal's religion to hold a condom

Karris We've done this, miss, we did it year eight

Zoe Well apparently there were four pregnancies in year eleven last year and one in year nine

Mickey Who was that?

Sal Jenna Hayes with the funny eye

Zoe Alright, who's going to put the condom on?
  Not *on* obviously, on the dild— I mean the –

Mickey Aha! Miss said dildo!

Zoe I mean on the prosthetic penis, I did not say dildo

Mickey You did, miss called it a dildo!

Zoe Alright, alright, who's going to do it –

Sal Don't look at me

Mickey Give it here!

Zoe Alright

Mickey Bit of experience with this sort of thing

Karris Not what I heard

Mickey What's that supposed to mean?

Sal Means you never use a skin

Mickey How would you know?

Karris When you shagged Louise Kendall

Sal Miss, he was shitting himself a few months back

Mickey This is bullshit

Sal See, miss, he's denying it before he even said nothing, that's a giveaway

Mickey No, it's not

Sal Surprised your dick hasn't rotted with Aids the amount of shagging you do, dirty bastard

Zoe Okay, I don't want to hear / it

Karris 'I'm too young to be a dad!'

Mickey Just 'cause your nine kids went straight in the incinerator

Zoe Mickey, put the condom on the prosthetic penis or get out

Mickey rips open a condom wrapper with his teeth.

Right, what's Mickey done wrong?

Sal Been born

Daniel Not supposed to use your teeth

Zoe Exactly

Mickey What's wrong with using your teeth?

Daniel Might rip it

Mickey You have to use your teeth

Zoe Why do you have to use your teeth?

Mickey You need one hand free

Zoe Why d'you need one hand free?

Mickey So you can be fingering the lady at the same time

Sal Oh my days

Mickey You need to get her all wet otherwise you break yer nob off going in

Sal So disgusting

Mickey (*sings*) Sophisticated lover!

Karris You go down on it?

Mickey Sophisticated, not gay like

Zoe So you open the condom with two hands, tearing down the side taking care not to rip it

Mickey Yeah, but in the heat of the moment it's not like that

Zoe The whole point of this is to make sure that even in the heat of the moment you take precautions

Mickey How am I going to remember all this when I'm drunk?

Zoe Well, hopefully, you won't be drunk, Mickey, and neither will the girl

Mickey How am I going to get her to take her knickers off if she's sober?

Zoe Oh my God

Daniel That is wrong, man

Mickey What?

Karris Miss, I would like to apologise on behalf of Mickey

Sal Such a dickhead, should be sterilised

Zoe I'm just going to pretend I didn't hear that

Mickey It was a joke, I'm joking

Zoe Who else wants a go?

Mickey Can't take a joke

Sal Don't look at me

Karris I'm not touching that

Zoe Daniel?

Mickey He'll probably try and stick it up his arse

Maz Mickey

Zoe Mickey, that's your final warning. (*To Daniel.*) You want to have a go?

Daniel Why don't you have a go, miss?

Karris Yeah, go on miss, show us how it's done

    Beat.

Zoe Alright, me first, then you. Which one shall I put on? Karris, will you pick one?

Karris Strawberry

Sal Why's it got a flavour on it?

Mickey Why d'you think?

    Zoe unwraps the condom.

Zoe See, not using your teeth

Karris Like your nails, miss. What, they're nice!

Zoe Make sure you pinch the teat, dispel the air

Zoe unfurls the condom over the prosthetic.

Then unfurl it down, taking care not to rip it

Maz Don't forget to breathe, Mickey

Sal There is no way I'd put that in my mouth

Karris Why? Is it not halal?

Zoe Tah-dah!

All applaud.

Karris What you think, sir? You enjoy watching miss do that?

Maz Highly educational

Karris takes the prosthetic and opens another condom.

Mickey They your own, miss, or you buy 'em special?

Maz I don't think that's –

Zoe Mickey, you're doing well, don't spoil it (it's my class, thank you, sir)

Sal Look at him, little perv

Daniel Yeah, I know someone won't be needing the internet for a week

Mickey Remind us, Danny, who's your favourite gay porn star again?

Daniel You are

Sal/Karris Ohhhh!!

Sal Why you in a laundry bag, Mickey?

Mickey Laundry bag?

Karris 'Cause you got taken to the cleaners!

Mickey Yeah, yeah, very funny

Zoe Mickey, ignore them. Daniel don't wind him up, you know he's a sensitive soul

Karris Here you are, sir, get a load of this

With a well practised movement, Karris rolls the condom over the prosthetic using her mouth.

Mickey Woah!

Mickey and Daniel clap. Maz begins to, but quickly realises he probably shouldn't.

Karris Thank you, thank you, and for my next trick –

Sal You are such a slag

Karris Can you do that, miss?

Zoe Not in term time

Karris Can you though, miss?

Zoe I'm not answering that

Maz That means yes, by the way

Zoe Somewhere you're supposed to be, sir?

Pause.

Karris Bye, sir

Maz I'll see you later, miss

Karris When you taking us for PE again, sir?

Exit Maz.

Karris Oooh! That was cold, miss, you slapped him right down!

Sal Think he likes you, miss

Zoe You reckon?

Karris Still got the hots for yer

Zoe To be honest, Karris, I'm out his league

Karris, Sal, Mickey, Daniel erupt with delight.
Exit Sal, Karris, Mickey, Daniel.
Enter Harry. He sneaks up on Zoe and grabs her.

Harry Ha!

Zoe Bloody hell, don't do that

Harry Word on the street is you're outstanding

Zoe What?

Harry 'S what Maz says anyway, he rates you very highly, which is saying a lot coming from Maz, 'cause he knows what he's on about

Zoe Does he?

Harry And he thought you were outstanding

Zoe All a fucking joke this, isn't it?

Harry Sorry?

Zoe Just one big fucking boys' club, sharing titbits, sharing the gossip, thinks I'm outstanding does he?

Harry Hang on –

Zoe Well, I'm so glad to have passed the test, I mean what am I rated on exactly? What are the categories? Foreplay for instance, quality of underwear, number of orgasms?

Harry Ah. Um. More to do with his role as your learning mentor, he's rated your teaching outstanding for this term. Good to outstanding actually, he says your classroom management skills have improved vastly, your lessons are well structured with excellent differentiation to ensure that all abilities are challenged – I'm paraphrasing – and the learning, on the whole, remains active throughout. Crossed wires, I think

Zoe Excellent. I'm pleased, obviously

Harry How's the Christmas do coming along?

Zoe Was that awkward for you too?

Harry You didn't take my advice then?

Zoe Wish I had

Harry Listen, keep it up, I mean – you've come a long way, I'm pleased
   Sorry about the grabbing thing, my partner told me I looked jaded, I was trying to be a bit more dynamic. Exciting times

   Daniel enters.
      Harry exits.

Zoe Daniel, have you got a moment?

Daniel Did you read my poem?

Zoe Oh God, yes, sorry, it's in the –

Daniel No, no, keep it

Zoe You've got a copy?

Daniel In here – (*Taps his head.*)

   Pause.

Zoe Yeah, it was good. What was that last line, um – 'Empty hearts and . . .'

Daniel 'Hateful eyes'

Zoe The way you swap the alliteration over, that's –

Daniel I know you write poetry so it means a lot

Zoe I'm glad. Listen, do you remember that detention with Mickey when things got a bit funny and . . . This is – do you remember Mickey saying 'Two against one, miss?'

I mean he said, 'Two against one,' do you remember that?

Daniel Yeah, I think so

Zoe What did he mean by that?

Daniel What do you think he meant?

Zoe That's what I'm asking you. I mean, do you think – I mean, well was it – was it a threat?

Daniel Could be, yeah

Zoe But was it?

Daniel Yeah, I suppose, yeah

Zoe What kind of threat do you think it was?

Daniel Miss, he said it to you, not me

Zoe What I mean is do you think it could have been . . . sexual?

Daniel Do you think it was sexual?

Zoe The thing is, I'm writing this report about it, and I don't want to overblow it

Daniel You want me to back up your story?

Zoe I don't want you to lie

Daniel You want me to back up your story?

Zoe Well, yes. It might not even come to that, it probably –

Daniel Fine

Zoe It probably won't

Daniel It's fine

Zoe You understand what I'm saying, I'm not wanting you to say anything –

Daniel I get it, it's okay

Zoe You do?

Enter Karris.

Karris Alright, miss, looking forward to Christmas?

Zoe Very much so

Karris Y'alright, Danny. You going Kelly's party?

Daniel Don't know

Karris Maybe I'll see you there, yeah?
See ya, miss

Exit Karris.
 Exit Daniel.
 Music. Harry, Zoe and Maz change into school uniform. Zoe enters. She smokes, drinks red wine. Daniel, Mickey and Karris change to look older. Enter Maz.

Maz No smoking on school property

Zoe offers him a cigarette.

I don't smoke

Zoe Neither do I

He takes a cigarette, lights it from hers.

Thanks for the assessment

Maz You earned it

Zoe What does that mean?

Maz Nothing

Zoe I fucking did earn it

Maz Joke

Zoe This place

Maz What?

Zoe I was temping in the depot for a maintenance company, they had the contract for the underground. Track boys came in every morning, sign off after the night shift. While they waited for the boss, they'd log on to a computer and look at porn. Zo, come and look at this, it's a monkey fisting a badger. Twats, the lot of them, always fighting, stick porn on your desk, the lot

Maz Sounds familiar

Zoe But I've never had someone say fuck off right to my face in my place of work

Maz Sure

Pause.

Zoe When I was fifteen I used to smoke draw in the girls' loos at school. I got arrested for assault once. Some bloke started on my boyfriend, so I started on him, then his girlfriend started on me and I lamped her. I went to court. Case got thrown out, she was such a fuckwit she couldn't even tell the truth without sounding like a liar
   Don't think you know me
   The other day I took a class and for the entire fifty minutes, they worked. They listened. They answered questions. No one slagged anyone off. It was amazing
   Couldn't have done it without you

Maz Yeah, you're probably right

Zoe Cheeky twat. You'll get this over you, you're not careful

Maz You wouldn't dare

A beat. Zoe tips her wine over Maz.

What's up with you?

Zoe You dared me

Maz Fuck's sake

Zoe Ahhh, did I mess up your school uniform? Will your mum be angry?
You in a mard?

Maz You complete mentalist

Zoe Best make it up then

Enter Harry.

Harry Jez Friday's hotwired the digger!
The yellow digger, Jez Friday, he's hotwired it. You know, the digger for the astro

Zoe Yeah

Harry Used to be a builder, he's hotwired the digger, he's taking it for a spin round the playing field

Zoe Serious?

Maz Now?

Harry It's brilliant, he's giving rides in the bucket, it's my favourite thing in my life ever! You coming?

Zoe Harry, you drunk?

Harry Drunk, no, I'm absolutely cunted. What you doing in here? Don't tell me, life's too short. I'm gonna ride in the yellow bucket!

Exit Harry.

Maz Let's go and join the others

Zoe Oh no you don't

Maz What?

Zoe I'm not asking you to be my boyfriend
    It's Christmas

Maz Who am I, fucking Santa Claus?

Zoe You've been trying to fuck me all term

Maz I already did, twice
    I didn't mean –

Zoe Oh I get it, part of a collection am I, like football
stickers, how many till you get the set?

Maz We had a bit of fun alright, it weren't that memorable

Zoe I gave you the time of your life

Maz You were eager, I'll give you that

Zoe You prick

Maz Look, I'm not your fiancé. Sorry, that came out –

Zoe Know what your problem is?

Maz I didn't mean –

Zoe You can't handle a real woman, just 'cause I'm not
one of your lobotomised dolly birds, hanging off your
every word

Maz Zoe –

Zoe Ooh, Maz, you're so sexy, Maz, you're so clever.
Only reason they think you're so great is they're fucking
children and too stupid to know better
    And you dare turn up at mine with a hard on I'll slam
it in the fucking door

Exit Zoe.
  Exit Maz.
  Enter Daniel. Enter Karris, carrying a bottle of vodka. They are in a garden.

Karris What you doing, mystery boy? Waiting to be found?

Daniel Maybe I don't want to be part of the crowd

Karris Only reason people sit on their own at parties is to get noticed. Want to blend in, you go with the crowd
  I'm trying to be nice

Daniel Get blown out by yer dealer mates?

Karris They ain't dealers

Daniel No

Karris Just sell a bit of drugs is all

Daniel Why you hang out with them?

Karris They got cars

Daniel That's the reason?

Karris I don't like walking
  I ain't clever like you, Daniel. I know what I got, I know why boys like me. Want some booze? Mickey nicked it from the teachers' stash for their party. It ain't poisoned

  Daniel takes the bottle and drinks.

Ever wish your life was different?

Daniel Yeah

Karris There's things I want so much I can never have

  Enter Mickey.

Daniel Yeah

Karris I'd love to ride a horse
  You got nice eyes

Mickey You want to ride a horse, do you? ride me like a pony if you like?

Karris Fucking stalker

Mickey Hey, who said you could drink my booze?

Karris I said he could

Mickey The fuck are you looking at?

Daniel Nothing

Mickey Fucking gayboy, 's what I thought

Daniel No. I'm looking at nothing. 'Cause that's what you are. A nothing no-good streak of shit and I don't even care what you do to me, 'cause it won't change the fact you're a sadsack with a big mouth and nothing to say

Mickey I'm looking at a dead man walking, son

Daniel Come on, badman, fuck me up then. Or you gonna be a washed-out pussyboy like your thieving old man?

Karris Oh fuck. Mickey, no. Mickey! Get off him! Get off him!

  Mickey hits Daniel again and again.

Daniel That all you got? That all you got?

Mickey Don't ever fuckin talk about my dad, you get me? You get me? You get me?

  Exit Mickey.
    Daniel's face is bleeding.

Karris Fucking hell, Danny

72

Daniel I'm know exactly what I'm doing

Karris Dan, we need to get you to A and E

Daniel I know exactly what I'm doing. I always know
what I'm doing!

> *Exit Daniel.*
>   *Exit Karris.*
>   *Enter Zoe. She is in her flat. The music is loud. She
> dances wildly, drinking from a bottle of spirits. Door
> buzzer. Door buzzer again.*

Zoe Wanker

> *Door buzzer. Zoe tries to ignore it, but can't. She takes
> a swig, exits and returns.*
>   *Enter Daniel, blood on his face, as before, perhaps
> a little worse. We barely hear them over the music.*

Daniel, what you doing here, you can't –
  What happened to your face?
  Who did this? Who did this to you?

> *They are very close.*

Spring

Enter Zoe, Mickey, Sal, Karris, Daniel.
  Mickey on top of a table.

Mickey You'll drop me

Zoe We won't

Mickey What if I land on my head?

Daniel It's already got a dent, one more won't make a difference

Mickey Put a dent in your head

Karris Go on!

Sal Bucurck!

Mickey Shut up

Sal Buck buck burcck!

Zoe Sal, that's not helping

Sal Sorry, miss

Zoe Mickey, we promise to catch you

Karris Haven't got all day

Mickey Fuckin' better do

Zoe We will, won't we, guys?
  Won't we?

Karris Ohh go on, you'll be safe with us you big wally

Mickey Bunch of dicks the lot of you

Sal Chicky chicky buck buck / burckkk!

Maz enters.

Mickey Fuck off, you gaylord

Sal Who you calling gaylord, dildo

Zoe Come on, focus. The whole point is Mickey needs to feel confident we'll catch him

Sal Jump. Jump

All join in.

All Jump, jump, jump, jump, jump, jump, jump, jump

Mickey Fuck it, it's stupid anyway

Sal Ohh, he's chickening out

Mickey climbs down.

Mickey No I'm not I just know you'll drop me

Zoe Alright, he doesn't have to do it. Fancy a go, sir?

Karris Go on, sir, I'll catch yer

Maz I think miss should have a go

Sal Oh yeah, that'd be classic

Maz Come on, miss, you up for it?

Karris Shall I have a go?

Mickey Yeah miss, go on

Karris Daniel, shall I do it?

Sal Yer fancy him or something?

Karris Shut up

Zoe Okay, okay, but you've got to promise to be careful

Zoe climbs on to the table.

Mickey Alrighty! Looking forward to this, sir?

Maz Behave!

Mickey I'll take this position

Sal Urrggh, don't be disgusting

Mickey (She could land right on it)

Zoe Make sure you're close in

Karris Daniel, you stand here

Mickey (Straight on it, uh)

Maz Mickey

Mickey (Makes my dick hard just thinking about it)

Daniel What, like you think you got a chance?

Mickey More chance than you

Zoe Daniel, concentrate, I'm relying on you

Zoe removes her shoes.

Mickey Concentrate, Daniel

Zoe Someone take my shoes

Daniel I'll take 'em

Zoe hands Daniel her shoes.

Mickey Yeah, take 'em home and wear them – with your ladies' panties you like to parade round in

Daniel What, the ones that belong to yer mum?

Sal Ah-hah!

Karris Shame! You got shamed there, boy!

Mickey No I didn't

Zoe You lot ready?

Karris Yeah!

Maz Any last words, miss?

Zoe Just bloody catch me

Zoe falls backwards. They catch her.

Karris Nice one

Sal How was that, miss?

Zoe That was actually really good

Karris Oh miss, you're a star

Sal Way lighter than Daniel

Mickey That's 'cause miss works out

Sal How do you know?

Zoe Mickey, would you mind removing your hand from my bum

Mickey Sorry miss

Sal Such a little perv

Karris You want a go, sir?

Daniel hands Zoe her shoes.

Yeah, sir, go on, have a go. I'd make sure I was underneath yer

Maz Not this time

Karris Oh go on, sir, be ever so gentle

Maz Not today thanks, Karris

Karris Why? Something big come up?

Maz Miss, can we have a word after?

Sal You asking miss out on a date, sir?

Karris Gonna treat her better than last time?

Zoe That's fine, sir

Karris/Sal Oo-ooh!

Exit Sal, Mickey, Karris, Daniel.

Maz You look confident

Zoe I feel confident

Maz Seeing someone?

Zoe Wouldn't you like to know

Maz I would, actually

Zoe Too late

Enter Daniel.

Maz Harry wants a word

Zoe Well, he knows where to find me

Exit Maz.

Daniel Miss

Zoe Sorry, Daniel, I'm in a rush

Daniel You're always in a rush

Zoe Is it important?

Daniel We need to talk

Zoe I think we've said everything that needs to be said

Daniel Yeah, but after what happened –

Zoe Nothing did happen

Enter Karris.

Daniel When can I see you?

Karris Miss, you got a minute?

Zoe No

Karris Want me to come back later?

Daniel When?

Zoe Daniel

Daniel When?

Zoe Tuesday, you can have the tutorial Tuesday, Daniel

Daniel After school?

Zoe Yes

Exit Daniel.

Karris Miss, I ask you something?

Zoe I'm sorry, Karris, I've got marking

Karris Where do you get your hair done?

Zoe What?

Karris Your highlights. They're really nice

*Enter Maz and Harry. Harry carries typed papers.
Exit Karris.*

Harry We're impressed

Zoe Thank you

Harry Maz's feedback is excellent (professional feedback, I hasten to add). Apparently you can teach

Zoe I know
Well, what am I supposed to say, 'No I can't'?

Harry Sorry, straightforwardness throws me. I'm much more comfortable masking my raging ego under a thin veneer of self-deprecation, it's a consequence of attending one of the minor public schools
How's things, how's tricks?

Zoe Well, the room, if you can call it that, is still freezing, my feet are killing me, my back hurts, I've taken up smoking again, the furniture's broken, I'm out of stationery and I'm an alcoholic

Harry Well, that's your professional development out the way

Zoe Though I would like to swap the citz group

Harry It's only till half term, then we're into exam groupings

Zoe Can't Maz take it?

Maz Got an options group now, sorry

Harry I thought you were getting on with them

Zoe I just like to teach my own subject that's all
    That it?

Harry Do you want Yvonne's job?

Zoe She's on maternity

Maz Silly cow's fault for getting knocked up in the first place. Joke

Harry She wants to be a full-time mum. We all thought she was a lezzer, got the shock of our lives, we assumed she had it inserted or whatever, but apparently she has a boyfriend. Anyway, she was talking to Sheila and it's not official but she's not coming back. Which suits us, she was shit anyhow and it's a right pain in the arse having to recruit

Zoe I thought you had to interview

Harry We'll get some idiot in, give them the tour, have a chat, tell them to fuck off. You're not going to get up the duff are you?

Zoe What?

Harry You're not going to get preggers?

Zoe You're not allowed to ask that

Harry I'm not allowed to buy booze for the Christmas party out of the training budget but fuck it, I've a school to run

Zoe You mean my training budget?

Maz It's not *your* training budget

Zoe The school gets a grand for taking me on, specifically for my training

Harry We didn't think we could keep you on

Zoe I wanted to go on a course

Maz What course?

Zoe 'Rights in the Workplace'

Maz You're joking?

Harry Yes, Maz, I think she is joking. Look, do you want this job or not?

Zoe Yes

Harry Great, it's yours, pending a few – you know, details

Zoe There's something else, isn't there?

Harry It that obvious?

Zoe Yes

Harry Your report. About the minor incident last term. I've read it

Zoe You've had that weeks

Harry Look, amidst the administrative nightmare that comprises nine-tenths of my life, I do occasionally try and squeeze in some teaching

Maz The allegation you've made is quite serious

Harry That's what I was building up to

Zoe Well, it was serious

Harry Well, yes, but you've made it sound very serious

Zoe It was

Harry You made it sound like Mickey made a, a, a, a –

Maz A sexual threat

Harry One of those

Zoe He did

Harry Did he?

Zoe Yes

Harry Did he really though?

Zoe All I did was write down what he said

Harry See, that's the thing, if you'd done that your report would have said, Mickey O'Shea said to me: 'Two against one, miss, what you going to do?'

Zoe It does

Harry No, what your report says is, 'Mickey O'Shea made a thinly vciled sexual threat, referring to the fact there were more of them than there was of me and they could overpower me.' And then you quote him. See, what you've done is interpreted the remarks in a very specific way

Zoe But that's what he meant

Harry How can you be sure?

Zoe What else could he have meant?

Maz You'd just told Mickey off

Zoe Yes, for making inappropriate remarks

Maz The innuendo about the dog

Zoe Yes

Maz So maybe he was disputing your interpretation of that. Maybe he was saying two against one to mean him and Daniel would both back up the fact that you'd misinterpreted the innuendo

Zoe But I didn't misinterpret the innuendo

Maz No, but I'm saying that might be what he was disputing

Zoe This is getting very convoluted

Harry If you accuse Mickey O'Shea of making a threat of sexual assault he could get a criminal record

Maz Is that what you want?

Zoe I'm not wanting to get anyone in trouble

Maz You know what Mickey's like, he just talks shit, he doesn't know what he's saying half the time, and forgive me, but if you really thought he was going to sexually assault you, would you really have gone back into the classroom with him?

Zoe You want me to lie on the form

Maz No

Harry We just want you to excise some of the words

Maz Harry

83

Harry Sorry

Maz We're asking you to consider whether it's more appropriate, more accurate in fact, to omit the conjecture and focus instead on what he actually said

Harry The conjecture kind of jumps out at you

Zoe This request to reconsider my sloppy use of language, this wouldn't by any chance have any bearing on Yvonne's job?

Maz They're entirely separate

Harry Though obviously it might be tricky you being here if the school's being turned over for its lax disciplinary procedures. (Ofsted have kind of asked to see our paperwork, it's a requirement of getting out of special measures)

Maz Plus we should have reported this to the police

Harry I was coming to that

Zoe So that's what this is about

Maz My main concern is Mickey

Zoe Of course

Maz He's a few months away from leaving, probably no GCSEs, army might be his only option, but he can't have a disciplinary problem

Zoe He's already got a disciplinary problem

Maz Not like this. Is that really what you want?

Zoe No

Maz Well then, maybe –

Zoe I might need some time to think about this

Maz Take as much time as you need

Harry Absolutely, although how much time do you think you will need?

Maz I think she'll take as much time as she needs, Harry

Harry She's laughing. Why's she laughing? That makes me uneasy, is that good or bad?

Maz She's laughing at us, you muppet

Harry Us, why's she laughing at us?

Zoe You arrange to meet me and then harass me into changing the wording of a report

Harry *Harass*, now come on

Zoe To cover your own arses and offer me a job as a sweetener

Harry That's a very, you know, way of looking at it

Maz Did you really think she was going to be okay with a bribe?

Harry Let's not say bribe, it's not a bribe

Maz What is it then?

Harry An incentive

Zoe You could make me Head of English

Harry English already has a head

Zoe Not next year

Harry Why not?

Zoe Corinne's taking your job

Harry How do you know I'm leaving?

Maz Everyone knows you're leaving

Harry I thought it was a secret

Zoe Did you tell him?

Harry Yeah
  Do the kids know?

Maz Course the kids know, kids know more than we do

Harry Bollocks, I was hoping to manage that

Zoe I don't think they care

Harry Thank you, but I think they'll find my departure highly disruptive

Maz I don't think they give a shit

Harry Yes they do. A bit. Don't they?
  Fuck

Maz You can't just make her Head of Department

Zoe Why not?

Maz What happens if you get a better candidate with more experience?

Zoe Thank you

Harry I will make a persuasive argument on Zoe's behalf

Maz Like what?

Harry The other candidate, having more experience, will cost more

Maz Tony and Anne have been here longer

Harry Well, in this case we'll opt for youthful enthusiasm

Zoe I am here

Harry And I think you'll find Maz that's 'two against one', if you catch my meaning

Zoe Fine

Harry offers Zoe a typed sheet of paper.

What's that?

Harry It's a retyped version of your statement

Maz You brought it with you?

Harry She doesn't have to use it, it's just there if she wants it

Zoe How do I know you'll keep your side?

Harry Because I'm a good and honest person and my word is gold
  You really won't get pregnant, will you? I mean, I know it's technically, you know, your 'right' and everything, but all joking aside, it would really bugger things up

Zoe No

Harry Smashing

Zoe Any other employment laws you want to violate today or . . .

Harry Ha ha, no, I'll leave the groping to Maz if you don't mind. Ah, I forgot about . . . I'll um . . . Oh! Either of you free first thing tomorrow?

Maz No

Zoe Why?

Maz Schoolgirl error

Harry I might need you to cover my politics lesson so I can oil the wheels so to speak, couldn't wing something, could you?

Zoe I don't know anything about politics

Harry They're all cunts. Sorry, you're right, that's childish and cynical, it's far more nuanced than that. Lib

Dems – feckless cunts. Labour – reckless cunts. Tories – total cunts. If they get stuck, get them to construct their own society through expressive dance, the mongs love that

Exit Harry.

Maz Alastair Campbell's got nothing on Harry, has he?

Enter Daniel, on the periphery, a different location.
He sends a text.
Zoe checks her phone.

Zoe D'you fancy a drink?

Exit Daniel.
Zoe and Maz are in the pub.
Zoe checks her messages intermittently.

I have done something unconscionable

Maz I'm a science teacher. What does unconscionable mean?

Zoe I sort of know what it means without being able to explain it

Maz looks it up on his phone.

Maz 'Not restrained by conscience. Beyond prudence or reason. Excessive. Unscrupulous'

Zoe Unconscionable

Maz You going to tell us then?

Zoe Can you keep a secret?

Maz What?

Zoe See that, 'What?' You say, 'Can you keep a secret?' someone says 'What?' you know they can't

Maz Now I definitely want to know

Zoe Exactly, soon as you know something no one else does, it's all you can think about

Maz The original sin, isn't it?

Zoe It's what you do with it though. *I love you. I don't love you. I'm leaving you. I'm seeing someone else.* Knowing something doesn't change a thing, but telling someone . . . and the moment before you tell someone, that moment, that's where you feel it, that little buzz

Maz Are you alright?

Zoe I can do this. I'm in control

Maz That the bloke you're seeing?

Zoe What makes you think I'm seeing someone?

Maz Checking your phone

> *Zoe is checking her phone.*

Cheers

Zoe What we drinking to?

Maz Head of Department

Zoe That bother you?

Maz Didn't realise you were ambitious is all

Zoe Ambitious. Ice-maiden
Maybe I won't change the report
How come my assessments are so good?

Maz You're a good teacher

Zoe That all?

Maz You can question a lot of things about me, but don't take the piss out my professional judgement. I do this job well, alright

Zoe Think you're a good person?

Maz Yeah, as it happens, I do

Zoe Don't you think it's odd how everyone thinks deep down they're a good person?

Maz No

Zoe Some of us must be bad. Look at us. All of it. I mean someone's doing the bad shit

Maz Not us

Zoe Other people

Maz I'm not saying I'm perfect, but – I work, well you know how many hours I work, I coach football, I recycle. Sort of. I do my bit. So do you. We all do

Zoe We all have this version of ourselves, the good version, that's us, that's who we are. But then we do something unconscionable. We have a problem. I'm a good person, so how could I do that, I'm not the kind of person to do that, but we are that kind of person. That's exactly the kind of person we are, that's exactly the thing we did but we can't just start admitting to ourselves that we're the bad people, can we? So we say 'That was out of character'. But there's no such thing as out of character, is there?

There's what we do. And that's it.

Oh my God

Maz What?

Zoe Just then. I almost said it

Maz Said what?

Zoe It

Not even the fear scares me any more. Look at that. Hair on my arms has stood up. I can feel it all down my

90

neck. The excitement, the thrill of it, like a charge. Boom, boom, boom

Maz I'm missing something

Zoe Why you here, Maz? Why you here, listening to me, listening to me talk shit?
That's the oldest story of all, isn't it?

Maz Shall I call us a cab?

Zoe No. I will

Enter Daniel.
Exit Maz.

Daniel We were supposed to meet

Zoe I was out

Daniel Where were you?

Zoe It's none of your business

Daniel You can't keep ignoring me

Zoe I'm not ignoring you, there's nothing to say

Enter Harry.

Harry Miss Curtis – hello Daniel – okay, if I observe?

Zoe Observe?

Harry One of your lessons, it's part of the, you know, the thing, I need to be able to vouch for your outstandingness myself

Zoe Can't you observe an English lesson?

Harry Timetable's squeezed me out, practicals, it's that time of year, Daniel would you mind, um –

Daniel What?

Harry Buggering off for a second. Please, of course, thank you.

Look, I've got to get a recommendation in before they get their minds set on someone else, and if it's not now, well that's it. Daniel, sorry, we're having a private conversation

Enter Karris, Mickey and Sal.
Daniel moves away.

Zoe Fine

Harry Have you looked at that report?

Zoe Not yet

Karris Hiya, sir

Harry (Hello!) Not to push, but, you know –

Zoe Fine

Mickey You alright, sir?

Harry Yes, Mickey, you?

Mickey I'm feeling very happy today, sir, very gay

Harry Well, how about your transfer your gaiety into a zen-like degree of focus on miss's excellent lesson?

Sal What we doing today, miss?

Zoe Carrying on with the worksheet

Karris Miss, you look unhappy, was you on one again last night?

Zoe distributes worksheets.

Zoe Okay, can we settle?

Mickey Are you testing miss, sir?

Harry No, but you're testing my patience, Mickey

Karris Miss is a dead good teacher, sir

Harry Glad to hear it

Zoe Can we settle down please?

Mickey Sir if miss is shit, does she get sacked?

Harry Okay, this is the last thing I'm going to say before miss carries on with her lesson. I don't want any showing off for my benefit. You might think behaving like animals is acceptable in my class but I'm sure miss doesn't stand for it, do you, miss?

Zoe No, sir

Harry And to answer your question, Mickey, no, I'm examining you oiks for signs of civility hitherto undetected

Mickey What's he saying?

Sal He's saying shut your stupid mouth you thick shit

Mickey Up yours

Zoe Right, we're going to carry on –

Sal Such a spastic

Mickey Takes one to know –

Zoe *Quiet!*
Okay, who can tell me what we were talking about last week, the worksheets should jog your memory

Daniel We were talking about –

Zoe Karris has her hand up. Karris?

Karris We were talking about relationships, miss?

Zoe Very good, any advance on that?

Mickey Whether it's okay to feel someone up

Karris Such a div

Mickey It's what we were talking about

Karris In your head

Zoe Okay, it's not exactly what I had in mind, but you are in the right area

Daniel That's what girls say to Mickey when he feels them up. 'It's not exactly what I had in mind, but you are in the right area'

Karris Ha!

Zoe I don't find that funny

Karris Sorry, miss

Mickey Least I prefer girls, sorry sir, no offence

Sal We were talking about boundaries

Zoe Good, Sal, someone tell me what a boundary is

Daniel It means the edge of something

Zoe Hands

Daniel puts his hand up. Karris has her hand up too.

Karris

Karris It's like something you don't want to do

Mickey What you don't want to do is quite a short list

Daniel Least she's got the option

Mickey Was I talking to you?

Karris Don't think I won't smash your little face in

Mickey Like to see you try

Karris Thanks, Daniel

Zoe Who can give me an example of a boundary?

Sal Some people choose not to sleep with people till they're married, that's a boundary

Mickey Fuckin' travesty is what that is

Zoe That's a really good example, Sal

Daniel How come she gets to answer when she doesn't put her hand up?

Zoe The important thing is we all have boundaries of one sort or another

Mickey 'Cept Karris

Karris Will you shut up?

Sal Give it a rest, bigmouth?

Zoe Okay, Mickey, I warned you, that's a detention

Mickey You did not warn me

Zoe I did warn you, Mickey

Mickey You're supposed to give me a warning!

Zoe Don't answer back, I did give you a –

Mickey Such bullshit

Zoe I will not have you talk to me like that

Mickey Fuckin picked on all the time

Sal Oh, you're breakin' my heart

Karris mimes, rubbing her thumb and forefinger together.

Karris Know what that is?

Mickey The world's smallest violin playin' just for me, yeah, I've not heard that before

Daniel No, it's you having a wank, actually

Sal Ah-ha!

Mickey You'd fuckin love that wouldn't you, love to watch me havin a wank, you fuckin queer

Zoe Mickey, count to ten. Daniel, any more, you're going straight to the head

Daniel Yeah, and I wonder what we'd talk about

Zoe Now if you look at your worksheets, there are four boxes –

Mickey How come he gets away with that?

Zoe If you look at the worksheets I have given you –

Mickey If I'd said that, I'd have been straight to the head

Zoe I have no problem spending the rest of the lesson copying out of books in silence, if that's what you want, that's fine by me

Mickey Such bullshit

Karris Miss, I don't want to do writing, it's well boring

Zoe Sal, read the first example

Sal 'Kieron's parents are away and he has invited Rochelle over to their house.'

Mickey Tt-tt-tt

Sal 'He has been putting pressure on Rochelle to have sex with him all week.'

Mickey Naughty Kieron

Zoe Ignore him

Sal 'Rochelle is not sure if she is ready yet but is worried that all her friends have lost their virginity and she has not. Rochelle is fourteen and Kieron is fifteen. Should she accept the invitation and if so, should she have sex with Kieron or not?'

Zoe Well read

Sal Thanks miss

Zoe So what do we think?

Sal She shouldn't go over

Mickey Why?

Sal She's not ready yet

Karris What if she wants to?

Sal You're not supposed to have sex till you're sixteen

Daniel Why not?

Sal It's against the law

Mickey Better stop then

Karris Why's it against the law?

Mickey Government says so

Sal So having sex is bad, but starting a war is okay

Mickey Political!

Daniel That right, miss? Fifteen too young?

Zoe I'm asking what you think

Karris I think it depends how mature the person is

Daniel What does having sex actually mean?

Mickey What?

Daniel When we say 'have sex' what does that actually mean?

Karris What, you don't know?

Zoe That's a silly question

Harry Is it?

Mickey Everyone knows what sex is

Daniel I mean, is a blowjob sex?

Zoe No, it's different, it's –

Daniel It's oral sex

Mickey Exactly, it's not sex, it's oral sex

Harry So Mickey, are you saying that unless two people have intercourse, they can do anything they like and it's not sex?

Daniel What about lesbians?

Mickey They're great

Zoe Can we get back on track?

Harry I think he's making a serious point (sorry, miss)

Mickey shows Sal a clip on his phone.

Sal I don't want to see it!

Zoe Mickey, phone

Mickey Oh right, so he can talk all dirty, but I can't get my phone out

Zoe Give

Mickey No

Daniel The point I'm making is that sex isn't just intercourse. Otherwise all gay people are virgins

Mickey Unless you've taken it up the arse

Zoe Mickey, phone, now

Mickey I'm not giving you the phone

98

Daniel Just saying if a blowjob isn't sex, what is it?

Mickey It's what you do for your pocket money

Zoe Give me the phone

Daniel You avoiding the question, miss?

Zoe I won't ask again

Mickey Fine, I'll keep it

Daniel Why won't you answer, miss?

Harry Okay Daniel, leave it

Zoe I can handle this, thank you, sir

Daniel She won't even answer the question

Zoe Give me the phone

Mickey No

Sal Just give her the phone

Daniel Why is that, miss?

Zoe Give me the phone

Mickey No

Daniel Why is that?

Zoe *Give me the phone!*

Mickey Fine, take it

> *Enter Maz.*
> *Exit Karris, Sal, Mickey.*

Harry I represent SLT, Maz is Head of Pastoral. Now, have you got something to say?

Goodness sake, Daniel. Mickey I expect this from – you?

What's got into you?

99

Daniel Ask miss

Harry I'm asking you

Maz Is there anything you want to talk to us about, anything going on at home?

Harry Apologies first, sir, then we can indulge our latent liberal tendencies

Maz He might have something to talk about

Harry He can apologise first

Zoe I'm not sure this is helping

Harry An apology or an exclusion, Daniel, which is it to be?

Maz I don't think that –

Zoe Okay –

Daniel I am really and truly sorry for everything that happened. The whole thing was a mistake as far as I'm concerned

Harry You satisfied with that, miss?

Zoe Yes, let's leave it there

Harry Alright, we'll put this blip behind us, Daniel, you're a good lad and it would be a shame –

Daniel There is one thing

Maz What's that?

Zoe Daniel, if there's anything we can do to improve things, you must let us know. We do want to help, you know that, don't you? I mean, you can talk to us. Any time

Maz Was there something you wanted to say, Daniel?

Daniel No

Harry Alright, off you go

Exit Daniel.
  Exit Maz.

This doesn't help your case for Head of Department

Zoe You're saying you won't put me forward?

Harry I'm just saying, Zoe, I can bend ears, I can't get blood out of a stone

Zoe We had an agreement

Harry I know what we agreed. Just keep your nose clean

Exit Harry.
  Enter Daniel.

Zoe Why are you doing this?

Daniel Have you still got my poem?
  My poem, the one –

Zoe 'Empty hearts and hateful eyes', yes, Daniel, I can't have this hanging over me, not knowing if you're going to say anything
  What is it that you want?

Daniel I want to have sex with you again

Zoe What do you mean, again? There wasn't a first time

Daniel What was it then?

Zoe You know what it was

Daniel Why won't you say it?

Zoe What difference does it make?

Daniel So I don't feel like I'm going out of my mind, like I made it all up

Zoe But we didn't do anything

Daniel Just say what we did

Zoe What do you want, a running commentary? You burst into my flat, covered in blood, you'd been beaten up. I was drunk and emotional, things started to happen, I didn't mean for it to happen

Daniel But it did

Zoe You pushed me on to the sofa, you went down on me, you wanted sex I said we had to stop, I felt guilty and I – does that cover it?

Daniel I didn't push you on to the sofa

Zoe That's how I remember it

Daniel closes in on Zoe, insistent but not violent.

Daniel Please

Zoe No
No, Daniel

Daniel I want to have sex

Zoe I said no

Daniel You owe me

Zoe I *owe* you? I owe you? I don't owe you a thing

Daniel You owe me something

Beat.

Zoe Fine, okay, why don't you just fuck me right now then, is that it, then we're quits, are we? Fuck me once, then you'll leave me alone, is that what you're saying?

Daniel What would you do if I said I was going to the police?

Zoe The – What do you mean, the police?

Daniel What would you say if I said I was going to tell them what we did?

Zoe I'd say I hope you don't mean that

Daniel Well, what if I do?

Zoe Are you threatening me?

Daniel Maybe

Zoe Tell them then! Go to the police! If you're going to tell them, just tell them!

Daniel I'm just saying how do you think it would look? If I called the police. What do you think they would say, how would this look to them, if they burst in here, right now, how would that look?

Zoe How would it look?

Daniel Yeah, how do you think that would play?

Zoe It would look like an emotionally troubled black boy who's forced his way into his white female teacher's flat, and is threatening her

Daniel What?

Zoe You asked how it looks, I told you

Daniel I didn't force my way in here

Zoe The first time you did

Daniel You buzzed me in

Zoe I was expecting Maz

Daniel takes this in.

Daniel What's me being black got to do with anything?

Zoe Nothing

Daniel Then why say it?

Zoe Because you asked how it looks

Daniel What are you saying?

Zoe I'm just saying if you tell the police anything then –

Daniel Then what? Then what? You'll tell them a black boy tried to attack you, is that it?
It's your word against mine, who says they'll believe you

Zoe It's fucking Tilbury, Daniel, who do you think they'll believe?

Daniel You'd do that?

Zoe No

Daniel You'd accuse me of that?

Zoe Of course not
The point is I could do it, but I'm not going to –
The point, the point is I'm saying I know how it looks, I know what I could do, I know that I have that, that, that, that power, and I'm choosing not to use that because there's no need

Daniel So why say it?

Zoe Because I'm scared

Daniel Why, because I'm black?

Zoe No, because you threatened me with going to the police. You said you were going to the police, you threatened me with that, and I'm saying, I'm saying –
Daniel, you – you – I'm not – I mean I wouldn't do that, and I know you wouldn't do that

Daniel But you'd say I did to save your own neck

Zoe This is my career, my life
  You know I don't think that about you

Daniel I want my poem back

Zoe What?

Daniel I want my poem back

Zoe exits, fetches the poem, returns, hands it to Daniel.

This doesn't exist. This never happened, okay

Zoe I'm so sorry

Daniel What are you sorry for?

Zoe For hurting you

Daniel Hurting me. Hurting *me*?

Zoe I took advantage of you when you were vulnerable

Daniel What do you mean, vulnerable?

Zoe Your situation

Daniel My situation. I dealt with that my whole life. You think that makes me vulnerable, fuck you. You think I don't cope with bigger things than this every day. I don't give a fuck about my dad, the man left me and my mum with shit. You think I didn't clock you from day one, some flakey white bitch looking for a black boy with a heart of gold to make her own

Zoe No

Daniel What am I, your project?

Zoe I care about you

Daniel Do you love me?

Zoe No. I don't

Daniel Think I didn't know what I was doing when I came round? Think that prick Mickey could lay one finger on me I didn't let him. I taken plenty worse beats than that, man, that was nothing. I played you. You didn't play me, I played you. No one plays me, no one

Enter Karris.
Exit Zoe.

Karris Well, this is nice. Freezing my tits off, staring at Gravesend

Daniel Goes all the way up London this river. Then all the way out to the North Sea and then psshhh. Containers come from all over. See them lights, that's more coming in –

Karris D'you bring me out here to look at containers, Daniel, 'cause I've got to say, this ain't exactly what I had in mind –

Daniel Bring all sorts. Cars. Tea

Karris Asylum seekers. It's true, they found a load of 'em dead a while back. Imagine that, that must be shit. Imagine how shit your life must be to think Tilbury's a step up

Daniel You got a nice voice

Karris Fuck off

Daniel I think that

Karris No you don't

Daniel I do

Karris Do yer?

Daniel Yeah

Karris How come you know all this stuff?

Daniel Do I?

Karris The boats, all this

Daniel My dad told me

Karris Yeah, but you remember it, like that taxi thing, I'd never remember that

Daniel You liked that?

Karris Go left, go right, all the descriptions. Oh, Daniel, it was like your eyes was all lit up. I never really noticed you till then. Wish I'd had a dad like that

Daniel I told my mum about that, you know, that I did something in class people liked

Karris Bet she was proud

Daniel She laughed. Said he never took you up London. Yeah, he did, I said, remember. Nah, she said, he took you down the fort

Karris Here?

Daniel She followed him once. Watched him park up then another car pull in. Left me in the cab with a blanket and got in the car with this woman
    Fucking bullshit, all of it, only told me the runs so I'd fall asleep
    What kind of person does that?
    Mum tells me I'm just like him

Karris You're a good person, Daniel

Daniel You don't know that

Karris How can someone with eyes that pretty be bad?

Daniel You ever worry this is all there is?

Karris Fuckin' hope not

Daniel produces the poem he took back from Zoe. He hands it to Karris.

This for me?
  Will you read it?

Daniel
  'The cabbie says "Where to?"
  I don't care, long as I'm with you
  Streetlamps slowly disappear,
  Our only luggage, hopes and fears
  Away from all the lies we drive,
  The empty hearts and hateful eyes.'

Karris Who'd you write that for?

Daniel Girl I love

Karris Fuck off. Bet you show that to all the girls

Daniel Just you

Karris No you never

Daniel Why would I lie?

Karris To get in my pants

Daniel Doesn't mean I'm lying

Karris You ain't winding me up?
  I ain't worth it

Daniel Yeah you are

Karris Feel awful about what happened at Christmas, Danny – you know, with Mickey

Daniel Personality tax

Karris Personality tax?

Daniel Getting your head kicked in every once in a while. That's just the price you pay for being different round here, innit. It's like a tax on having a personality

108

Karris Your brain!
  Come on, tiger, you got a condom then or what?

Daniel Yeah

Karris Thought you might

  *Daniel produces a condom. Karris removes her
  underwear and arranges herself on the coat. Daniel
  undoes his trousers.*

Daniel Take my coat

Karris Hold steady
  You got a nice dick

Daniel Is it?

Karris That nice?

Daniel Yeah

Karris Put it on then

  Daniel begins to put the condom on.

Daniel Ah shit

Karris What? You haven't?

Daniel I tore it. Bollocks

Karris It's okay. We can still do it. I'll take the morning
after, I done it lots of times
  I ain't got nothing if that's what you're worried about

Daniel We could do something else

Karris This part your grand plan is it?
  You want me to suck you off, I don't mind

Daniel No, no, I meant something else

Karris You're not sticking it up me bum

Daniel Why don't I go down on you?

Karris You what?

Daniel I said why don't I go down on you?
  That is the first time I have ever seen you look shocked

Karris I'm not

Daniel You gone red

Karris I have not

Daniel Why you blushing?

Karris Don't know. No one's ever asked me that before

Daniel What you're not telling me you never . . .

Karris No. Well, yeah

Daniel You're joking me

Karris I'm not joking you, shut up

Daniel It's just funny that's all

Karris What you mean, I fucked so much but no one
ever done that?

Daniel I thought everyone did that

Karris Isn't it a bit . . . you know?

Daniel What?

Karris Disgusting?

Daniel No

Karris You done it before?

Daniel Yeah

Karris Who with?

Daniel This woman I was seeing

Karris Woman? How old was she?

Daniel In her twenties

Karris Fucking hell, you're a dark horse
D'you mind I'm younger than her?

Daniel No

Karris Feel embarrassed now

Daniel Lie back

Karris Feel nervous. Like being on the rides at Southend
'Cept they just make me sick

Daniel Relax

Karris I am

He goes down on her.

Daniel Stop laughing

Karris Sorry, it tickles, ah
Danny
Will you say that poem again?

Daniel Can you shut up a second?

Karris Sorry, I'm – Oh my days. She teach you that an'
all?

Mickey enters on the periphery, somewhere different.

Mickey (*graffiti, not spoken*)
In ths cold world u only luv
But one girl + I
Found her but she
Left me 4 Someon else

Exit Mickey, Daniel, Karris.
Enter Zoe.
Enter Harry.

Zoe Harry. Can you guarantee Head of Department?

Harry I can't guarantee it, Zoe / but I'll

Zoe I'll change the report. About the incident with Mickey. Can you guarantee it?

Harry I'll see what I can do

Enter Karris, Mickey, Sal and Daniel.
Exit Harry.

Karris Miss, you gonna miss us?

Zoe It's only half term

Karris But we're not seeing you after, are we?

Sal Course she's not going to miss us, she hates us

Karris No she doesn't

Sal Course she does

Zoe I don't hate you, Sal

Karris What, not even Mickey?

Zoe Not even Mickey

Karris Who will you miss the most?

Mickey Not me, that's for sure

Karris Is it me, miss?

Zoe I'll miss you all the same

Zoe hands out forms.

Karris Yeah, but you'll miss me the most, won't yer? It's alright you don't have to say, I know how it is

Mickey Fuckin' lesbian infatuation

Karris Shut up, what's up with yer?

Mickey It's fuckin' bullshit, just when I get a teacher I like, they always go. Now I'll have someone shit again

Zoe Sorry, did you just say you like me, Mickey?

Mickey No

Sal What's this?

Zoe These are feedback forms I'm handing out, so you can say what you think of me

Sal So we get to say whether we like you or not?

Zoe Yes, be nice – no, you can say what you like

Karris Miss, how do you spell fantabulosa?

Mickey It's not even a word

Karris I think it is

Sal Miss, what you doing over half term, you going away?

Zoe Sleeping

Karris I won't be doing much of that

Sal Get a room

Karris Oh we will

Mickey Keep it to yourselves

Karris passes Sal a piece of paper.

Sal What the fuck is this?

Karris (*sotto*) Daniel wrote it for me. (*Loud.*) Anyone see that programme on trannies in RE?

Mickey That was minging

Karris I thought it was sad, that girl's story made me cry

Mickey That was a boy

Karris Looked a bit like you

Mickey Fuck off

Sal Who wrote this?

Karris points at Daniel.

Zoe Can't do this sensibly, we'll be copying out

Mickey Let's see

Mickey snatches the poem. Karris pursues him as he reads excerpts.

Karris Hey

Mickey What is this?

Karris Give it

Mickey 'The cabbie says "Where to?"' What is it?

Karris It's mine, Daniel wrote it for me

Mickey Fuckin' love poem?

Karris Give it

Mickey
  'The cabbie says "Where to?"
  I don't care, long as I'm with you'

Oh that's nice

Zoe What's going on?

Karris You rip that I'll stamp on your fuckin head

Mickey 'Our only luggage' – Ow! – 'Hope and fears |
Streetmaps slowly' – Ow! Fuckin 'ell

Karris reclaims the poem.

Karris Wanker

Mickey Fuckin' scratched me, miss, nearly scratched my
eye out

Karris Scratch both your eyes out, little wanker

Mickey You hear that, miss? Load o' shite anyway

Karris It's not shit, you just don't understand poetry

Mickey Oh like you do?

Karris Miss knows, miss knows about poetry, that was good, wa'n't it? Wa'n't it Miss?

Zoe It's hard to tell on a first hearing

Mickey See, even miss thinks it's shit

Karris No she never, that's not what she said, she said she hadn't heard it

Zoe Daniel wrote that for you, did he, Karris?

Karris Yeah, 'cause he's my lo-verr

Mickey I could write better than that with my left hand

Karris Jealous much?

Mickey Of gayboy?

Karris Oh he ain't gay

Mickey Why would I be jealous of him?

Karris 'Cause he's Britain

Mickey He's Britain?

Karris And you know what Britain's got. Talent! And I ain't just talkin' 'bout the poem

Mickey As if

Karris He's better than you

Mickey How would you know?

Karris 'Cause he's experienced, he's been with an older lady

Mickey So?

Karris Well, she taught him some things that he taught me and I like 'em

Mickey You're such a liar

Karris Want to know what Louise Kendall said?

Mickey This is bullshit

Karris Want to know what she said about Mickey?

Mickey This is total bullshit

Sal She ha'n't even said anything

Mickey 'Cause I know she's going to lie

Karris She said, right –

Sal You're always doing that, denying it before she said nothing

Karris Louise Kendall said you came in about two seconds

Sal So obvious

Mickey Lies

Karris Made a right mess all over her, that's what she said

Sal Miss, you alright?

Karris She said you was a right lickle boy, you get me, not like Daniel

Zoe Alright, that's enough

Mickey She's a lying slag, just like you are

Karris Yeah, yeah, you need tips, two-second boy, Danny knows how to show a girl a good time

Mickey You're a liar

Karris No I'm not

Zoe Mickey –

Mickey You're just acting all sophisticated to / make yourself sound all grown-up

Zoe I'm asking you

Mickey 'Oh he's so great in bed, my life's just like *Sex in the City*'

Zoe Will you please shut up

Mickey You shut up, don't tell me to shut up

Zoe Do not talk to me like that

Mickey You're not allowed to tell me to shut up

Zoe I will talk to you how I choose

Mickey Why's it always me? Why do I get singled out?

Zoe I am not singling you out, I'm just trying to get some control

Mickey How come she's slagging me off, I'm the only one whose name you say?

Zoe Will you be quiet?

Mickey Urrrghh. Your breath stinks. What is that, curry? You been sucking Shagger Maz's cock again?

Sal Oh my God

Karris You can't say that

Mickey Say what I like, it's true

Daniel Leave her alone

Mickey Look, I know you mean well, but all things considered, fuck off back to your shit poetry and your alcky mum and your dad who left you 'cause he hated you and that's all there is to it

Zoe You stupid little boy

Mickey What?

Zoe You stupid idiotic, insignificant, good-for-nothing little boy

Mickey I'm not stupid

Zoe You've got nothing to give so all you do is pull others down to your own level

Mickey Why you always defending him? Why you always pick on me?

Zoe You talk about his dad. I've met your father

Mickey I swear to God, don't talk about / my father

Zoe Pathetic seedy little man. You know, we laugh about him, shambling around stinking –

Mickey I swear to fuckin' God –

Zoe I pity you, he's your father, but you know what I pity most? You're just like him. A gutless, talentless little good-for-nothing – as if you're ever going to achieve anything your whole life, Mickey. Did you hear Daniel's poem, did you listen, because at the end of that poem those people with the empty hearts and hateful eyes, that's you

Silence.

Oh my God. Oh my God, I'm so sorry, Mickey, that was a horrible thing to say, I'm so sorry. That was a horrible thing to say, I'm so sorry. I'm so sorry, I didn't mean it, I promise, I'm so sorry

Silence. Sal takes the poem from Karris's desk.

Sal Miss, how come you know the last line of the poem?

Zoe What?

Sal Just asking how come you know the last line. Said you never read it before

Karris No one's read it apart from me and Daniel, he wrote it for me

Mickey takes the poem.

Mickey How come she knows how the end goes?

Karris 'Cause you just read it out

Mickey 'Empty hearts and hateful eyes'. I didn't get that far, I only read the first two bits

Zoe No, you read the whole thing out. Mickey

Sal No, he didn't

Zoe No, he did, he read the whole thing out

Mickey I didn't get that far

Zoe Mickey, you made a mistake

Mickey Why you being all funny about it?

Zoe I'm not being funny about it, you made a mistake Alright, I don't know what you're suggesting. Mickey

Mickey I haven't suggested anything

Karris What you on about?

Zoe Nothing, he's not on about anything

Sal What?

Zoe Nothing

Mickey I haven't even said nothing, she's denying it, I haven't said a thing

Zoe I'm not denying anything, 'cause there's nothing to deny

Mickey He asked you for a kiss, this is hilarious

Zoe This is –

Mickey Look at her, she's gone bright red

Sal Miss, you are, you're blushing

Mickey He wrote that for you?

Zoe That is ridiculous

Mickey So how come you know what's in the poem?

Zoe You made a mistake. You made a mistake, you read it all out

Mickey No I never

Daniel 'Cause I showed miss the poem. I showed miss some of the poetry I wrote, that's how she knows

Karris You told me you didn't show anyone

Daniel I showed it to miss, just to see what she thought

Zoe Daniel showed me the poem, to ask me what I thought of it

Mickey You said you'd never read it before

Zoe No I didn't

Sal You said it's hard to tell first time you read it

Karris That's right, miss, you did say that

Mickey Why you lying? Why would you even bother?

Zoe You are crossing a line

Mickey He wrote that poem for miss

Sal Oh my days

Zoe You're making a . . . fool of yourself

Mickey Look at her. Look at them both. Deny it then

Zoe I'm not going to deny something as ridiculous as this

Mickey She won't deny it

Zoe Whatever you're implying is not true

Karris Chat so much shit, Mickey

Mickey Then why won't they deny it?

Zoe Fine. It didn't happen. You're being ridiculous

Karris Such a shit-stirrer

Mickey He's not denying it

Karris That's 'cause it's stupid
  Isn't it? Danny?
  You wrote this for me, didn't you?

  Pause.

Zoe Daniel?

Daniel Sorry

Karris Why you saying sorry?
  Danny?
  Why you say sorry for?
  Oh my God. It's her, isn't it? She's the woman you were talking about

Daniel No

Zoe No, Karris. you've made a mistake

Karris I feel sick. After the things you said, I thought you was different, but you're just like everyone else. I bet you was laughing about me

Zoe Karris –

Karris I trusted you

Zoe Karris –

Karris Don't say my name.
  You fucking slag, don't even say my name!
  Don't even say my name!

  Karris attacks Zoe. Sal runs out. She returns with Maz
  and Harry. They drag Karris out.
    Exit Sal, Mickey.
    Daniel and Zoe stare at one another.
    Exit Daniel.
    Enter Maz.

Maz Harry's with Daniel now. Fuck knows where Karris
and Mickey are. Police'll need to speak to you about
Karris

Zoe I don't want her to get in trouble

Maz She assaulted you, Zoe, doesn't matter what was in
her head, you can't just –
  If I've not looked out for you, I'm sorry. We all get a
bit caught up. Should have paid more attention
  Fucking hormones, eh?
  You alright?
  Never can tell if you're laughing or crying

Zoe What harm can it do?

Maz What harm can what do?

Zoe I mean . . . God you're a fifteen-year-old boy and
your relatively, no fuck it, your attractive teacher, then,
that's, I mean . . . I mean, there's no jobs or money or
anywhere to live and if that's not enough there's bombs
and drugs and guns and knives and nothing to live for,
but that's not what's really going to mess you up, is it?

Maz What?

Zoe You know maybe that's the problem, maybe that's what's wrong with the world, maybe that's what the men of this world need, someone to give them a proper fuck when they're fifteen, get it out their system, not just a fumble, I mean fuck algebra, that should be on the curriculum, sort out half the world's problems, wouldn't it?

Maz You saying it's true?

Zoe (*smiling*) What do you think, Maz? Honestly, what do you think, have I done something unconscionable? You think I've got it in me?

    Enter Harry. He sees Zoe smiling.

Harry All this about a poem, not even a very good one. Ah. Nice to see smiles. Zoe, I'm so sorry, and please, I know you must be angry, if you want to talk to your union I understand

Maz Harry –

Harry Actually, please don't talk to your union, not that I'm saying you can't, I'm just saying –

Maz Harry

Harry Yes

Maz She had sex with him

Harry I'm sorry, for a moment, I thought you said –

Maz I did

Zoe I didn't. Wish I had, but I didn't

Maz She had sex with him

Harry Is this true?

Zoe No

Harry Okay, then why are you saying she has?

Maz It's not just me. Two other students said she did

Harry And the student denies it, as does she

Maz She admitted it

Harry When?

Maz Just now, when you were out

Zoe I did no such thing

Maz All but. Are the police still here?

Harry Police?

Maz They can sort this out

Harry Sort what out?

Maz Maybe they'll find something, phone records, I don't know

Harry Based on what, Columbo? Your *hunch*?
What the fuck is going on? Is this one of your domestics, are you two off or on, you're worse than that fucking couple from the BT advert, 'cause I am harassed enough –

Maz I am going down the corridor to the police, this is too much to be smoothed over –

Zoe I didn't have sex with him

Harry No one's smoothing over anything, there's nothing to / smooth over

Maz You don't want the hassle 'cause you're leaving, you've got one eye on your pension, and / you know it

Harry I resent that

Zoe Is this 'cause I dumped you? Or the Head of Department thing? Can't be too ambitious, can we? Us ice maidens

Harry Oh God

Maz Your arrogance is breathtaking

Zoe *My* arrogance?

Maz Don't think I don't know what you're doing

Zoe What am I doing?

Maz You tell me, what are you thinking, you even know?

Zoe You want to know?

Maz Enlighten me

Zoe Well, it goes something like this. I'm thinking all the hours I've worked. I'm thinking how you left me with a class of the most difficult students, unsupported, during my NQT year
      I'm thinking you failed to protect me when a student threatened me with sexual assault and then asked me to change the report to cover your backs. And I'm thinking that you have taken me to the pub, got me drunk and engaged in crass and inappropriate sexual discussion about which students you'd most like to sleep with

Maz You joined in with that as / much as we did

Zoe Which I felt obliged to join in with because of the presence of my mentor and a member of the / senior leadership team

Maz That is bollocks and you / know it

Zoe Not to mention the persistent sexual harassment from my mentor who made continual attempts to get me into bed –

Maz I turned you down!

Zoe – with stories about his sexual prowess. And I haven't even touched on the wanton misuse and destruction of government property that occurred at the staff Christmas party. I think my union will be interested

Harry Well, it's nice to know someone's paying attention round here

Maz She has had sex with a student

Harry She says nothing happened. He says nothing happened. So nothing happened

Zoe I haven't had sex with anyone

Harry Alright, let's not go that far

Maz You think the school's reputation is more important than her being a sex offender?

Harry Don't say sex offender, that makes me very queasy

Zoe (*to Maz*) I would be very careful what accusations you throw at me, sir, because I will be repeating your exact words to my union representative and my lawyer

Maz Fuck the pair of you, the police don't want to know, I'll go to the papers, I'm sure they'll be very interested in what's going on at this school

Zoe Yeah and I'm sure they'd love to hear about you and Karris Jones

Maz What about me and Karris Jones?

Zoe How you sexually harassed her

Maz What?

Zoe How you gratified yourself sexually by rubbing your erection against her in a PE class and then boasted about it to other members of staff. I know I'm not the only one you told

Maz That was – that wasn't –

Zoe 'Have you seen her. Course I'd fuck her'

Harry Let's be honest, Maz, everyone's heard you say that, it's your party piece

Zoe How confident are you when I start trawling local nightclubs, and I will, I won't find anyone you've fucked that's under age?

Maz Harry. You know me?

Harry Yes, I do

Maz What does that mean?

Harry If someone asks me if I can corroborate you saying those words, and I know you meant them as a joke, but whichever way you cut it, saying you'd fuck a fifteen-year-old student whose arse you rubbed your cock against does not sound good

Maz She had sex with a student

Harry According to who? Two congenital liars and Don Juan of Tilbury, highly reliable
    Just *think* for a second. This conversation makes sense to us, fine, it's banter, we're letting off steam, we're talking about Karris Jones, but to anyone else, she's a fifteen-year-old girl

Maz Daniel made a pass at her earlier in the term. She told me that

Harry And as her learning mentor, what did you do with that information? Did you pass it on? Did you write it down? Did you raise it at the time?
    We go with the original report. Zoe's original report, we go with that. It's the more accurate version anyway

Maz That's not what you said before

Harry Well, it's what I'm saying now. She was there remember, we weren't

127

Mickey O'Shea threatened Zoe, that's why he lashed out today, that's why he concocted this story, he got wind that Zoe had submitted the report

Maz It's Zoe's word against Mickey's

Harry Exactly. And Daniel backs her version up

Maz How do you know?

Harry I asked him about it just now, he said Mickey threatened her

Maz You know Mickey'll get arrested

Zoe I don't want to press charges

Harry It won't come to that, but he won't be coming back. Neither will Karris

Maz You're fucking with these kids' lives

Harry As if they weren't fucked before they even set foot. Have you met Mickey's father, have you seen where Karris lives?

Maz We're supposed to help them

Harry We're not social workers, Maz, we're teachers, I've got a thousand other kids all needing my attention
  Karris assaulted a member of staff. Mickey sexually threatened a member of staff, these aren't angels

Maz Karris had good reason –

Harry And that makes it okay, does it? If you haven't noticed, we're short staffed as it is, what do you think happens when teachers start thinking it's okay for kids to assault them? And once all the teachers have gone, how many kids will we be helping then? Look at us – we're creaking. Straining at the seams, think we've time for lost souls, we've barely got time for the paperwork

Maz You don't care, do you? You just don't give a fuck

Harry DON'T YOU DARE TELL ME I DON'T CARE! EVER! Thirty-five years working miracles in the vain hope someone might get a job on the counter in Boots. So don't you dare tell me I don't care

Maz Don't think you've heard the end of this

Harry No, I think we have. By the way, you've made advanced skills, we're giving you a pay rise. Happy half term

Exit Maz.

I've always dreamt of working in one of those schools where you spend your days helping bright sixth-formers into Oxbridge

Zoe What are we doing?

Harry What are we doing? Giving them skills they don't need for jobs that aren't there, all in the hope that maybe, maybe when they're in charge they won't hate us so much they realise it's all a big lie and slit our throats in the night

Zoe I mean what are we doing now?

Harry I'll deal with the police, and Maz. The parents were mostly students of mine, they may think me a rambunctious old twat but for some reason in my presence they regress to twelve. I give them a bollocking, they'll pipe down

Zoe Thank you

Harry There's a job going in Kent, starts next term, not advertised yet. Less SENs, playing fields, all round a nice place to work. Oh, and it's single sex, girls. Boo-hoo. You'll get the job. Head's an old chum. Bit of sick leave, paid, put you on a few courses, see out the term that way.

There's one next week, you can go in my place. It's on the future of education

Zoe What if I don't want to go?

Zoe understands it's not a choice.

I'd better talk to the police

Harry Form reports

Zoe How do you do it for so long?

Harry Love, as they say, is blind. And contrary to my protestations, I'm rather fond of the little shits. Pension's not bad either
You can teach

Zoe Who'd have thought?